Thinking the Twenty-First Century

About the author

Dr Malcolm McIntosh FRSA has been teaching and writing on corporate responsibility and sustainability since 1990. He has worked at the universities of Warwick and Coventry, and has been a Visiting Professor at the Universities of Nottingham, Bath, Bristol, Stellenbosch, Doshisha, Waikato and Sydney. He has most recently been Professor and the Founding Director of the Asia Pacific Centre for Sustainable Enterprise at Griffith University in Queensland, Australia. He is the author or co-author of more than 27 books and numerous articles, and has been a frequent commentator on television and radio around the world on social issues, business responsibility and sustainable enterprise. He has been a Special Adviser to the UN Global Compact; worked for UNEP, ILO and UNDP; advised the UK, Canadian and Norwegian governments and global corporations, such as Pfizer, Royal Dutch Shell, BP and Unilever, and international NGOs. He is the Founding Editor of the peer-reviewed *Journal of Corporate Citizenship*. Previous careers include setting up and running English-language schools in Japan and Australia in the 1970s; peace research at Bradford University in the '80s; followed by ten years as a BBC TV journalist and film producer.

This wonderful book should be required reading for anyone who cares about building the new types of cross-sector and multi-disciplinary leadership skills, institutional structures and partnerships that are so urgently needed to drive more inclusive and sustainable prosperity. Malcolm McIntosh draws on his years of experience as a pioneering practitioner and scholar at the forefront of the global corporate responsibility and sustainability movement to give us a thoughtful, eloquent and passionate call to action. He challenges and inspires us in equal measure, and offers a compelling combination of historical evidence, current dilemmas and future vision to make his case for change. His work has already influenced thousands of students and practitioners around the world, and this book should encourage many others to take personal responsibility for building a better world.

Jane Nelson, Director, CSR Initiative, Harvard Kennedy School

---

When we have so much awareness of the rise of mindfulness and sustainability, this book is a hope, connecting the wisdom of East and West for our future on Earth.

Professor Mari Kondo, Director, Doshisha Business School, Kyoto, Japan

---

Malcolm McIntosh is not a designer, but *Thinking the Twenty-First Century* is an inspirational call to action for design that comes not a moment too soon. Taking us on journey through the changes we must make to our systems, our society, our institutions and our worldviews, it allows us to imagine and design a radically different future and provides the knowledge, the optimism and the courage to help us get there.

Clare Brass, Head of SustainRCA

It is rare to find an author willing to speak truth to power as McIntosh does in this thoughtful and provocative look at the ills of our present world and at ways to escape the inevitable outcome we face if we ignore their causes. He calls sustainability the illusion of progress that it is. Full of his own reckonings, it is hard to put down and slip back into inaction.

John R. Ehrenfeld, author of *Sustainability by Design*

A page-turner that synthesises the thinking about why we need to change, and how it might come about.

Sara Parkin, Founder Director, Forum for the Future

This thoughtful book by Malcolm McIntosh is a collection of five essays, each on a change required to build a new global political economy. Ranging widely from rebalancing science and awe, the impact of feminine thinking on peacefulness to quiet leadership, as well as more expected areas of earth systems and institutional reorganisation, each essay is a stimulating discussion drawing on a remarkable array of sources. Reading the book is like spending an evening in personal and invigorating conversation with someone who brings you new ideas or reframes things which you may think you know already. You come to know the author, appreciate his open self-awareness and his quiet wisdom; you will delight in the paradoxes that he illuminates – a very worthwhile experience.

Sir Mark Moody-Stuart, Chair, Foundation for the Global Compact; former Chair of Royal Dutch Shell and Anglo American

---

McIntosh urges us to bridge the thin line between a cosmological and a deeply intimate view of our circumstances and possibilities.

Simon Zadek, Senior Fellow, Global Green Growth Institute and the International Institute of Sustainable Development

---

Lots of fresh ideas in a way that is delightful to read. This book will more than repay careful thought, whether you agree with it or not.

R. Edward Freeman, University Professor and Olsson Professor, The Darden School, University of Virginia, USA

Malcolm McIntosh sees the twenty-first century in transformative terms. Five great currents of change, often turbulent and unpredictable, will frame the political economy of the future. Indeed, we can see signs of its arrival all around us today. These changes are, in brief: a global and holistic view of the world; the evolution of knowledge to rebalance science and awe; peacefulness and the rise of empathy and social cohesion, which he attributes to a feminisation of decision-making and governance; the new and varied ways we organise activities; and the power of adaptive learning.

The shape of the emerging political economy is being moulded by these five forces; Malcolm McIntosh brilliantly analyses and assesses the crucial elements of each. This is a book worth reading by a man worth knowing.

James E. Post, J.D., PhD, John F. Smith, Jr Professor in Management, Emeritus, Boston University, USA

'Brilliant' is a term that the British often use to describe something they like. I want to use that term in the more American sense to signify that this book is truly brilliant. Malcolm McIntosh, a polymath of the first order, combines science, politics, economics, feminisation and spirituality among other areas of insight in *Thinking the Twenty-First Century* to create a call for a new order that is much needed in our world. In words that pull few punches, McIntosh calls for five crucial changes: sustainability and awareness of globality; rebalancing science with awe – and spirituality; feminisation of the world to incorporate values of connection, caring and harmony; rethinking capitalism; and adopting a 'quieter' form of leadership. Read this book! You will be glad you did.

Sandra Waddock, Galligan Chair of Strategy, Boston College Carroll School of Management, USA

This is a book that challenges us to think about the big problems – the ones we too often hide from by focusing on our little corner of work and world; the ones that overwhelm us; the ones that seem too vast and intractable to even attempt to address. Recognising both the crushing weight as well as the absolute necessity to address these questions – questions of who we are as human beings, why we live and how we organise ourselves in ways that may allow us to continue as a species – Malcolm McIntosh has seemingly found a freedom in the very weight of these issues. He invites us to throw off the usual constraints of discipline-based thinking, allowing us to find a joy and intellectual freedom that can fuel us even as we stand, clear-eyed before the challenges that will determine our fate. McIntosh has given us all a gift: more than answers he has rather demonstrated a way forward.

Mary C. Gentile, PhD; author of *Giving Voice To Values: How To Speak Your Mind When You Know What's Right*

Thinking the Twenty-First Century is a magnificent, unruly, exuberant book . . . a book that traverses all the modalities of human thought and action to find practical wisdom in unlikely places. It offers us a viable and satisfying model for political and intellectual leadership . . . If the UN High-Level Panel on Global Sustainability really do want a transdisciplinary and cross-sectoral approach to a new political economy, then they could not want for a better guide.

Richard Little, Impact International Ltd

A burning man amidst the sociopathic ecopolitical landscape, this beautifully written book advocates for a balanced political economy with community at its centre, as an alternative to a world built to feed the system of neoliberal economics. The book is educating, witty and rich in history; much like a conversation with its author, it is bound to leave you feeling nourished and wanting more. Most of all, Malcolm McIntosh's book is a reminder that we *can* do things differently.

Renata Frolova, Head of Responsible Procurement, Maersk Line, Denmark

This book, partly diary and partly a collection of essays, is a love letter to life and encouragement not to go quietly but to scream loudly.

**David J. Vidal, Senior Fellow and former Head of Sustainability,
The Conference Board, New York, USA**

Malcolm McIntosh's consciousness-shifting book helps us see the problems that threaten our very human existence. I recommend it to anyone who is ready for a paradigm shift in leadership for the twenty-first century.

**Amina Aitsi-Selmi, Honorary Senior Research Associate, University
College, London, UK, MA (Cantab.) MRCP MPH MFPH PhD**

The world is becoming more and more dominated by specialists who know a lot about a particular topic. We desperately need people who have a wider focus such that they see the larger pattern of things – and Malcolm McIntosh is one of these special people. He combines this wider vision with experience at the top of global companies and media. For the reader, the combination of experience at the top and commitment to the future results in a book that is compulsive reading.

Alan Feest, Chartered Ecologist, University of Bristol, UK

Thinking
THE
Twenty-First Century

IDEAS FOR THE NEW POLITICAL ECONOMY

MALCOLM McINTOSH

Greenleaf
PUBLISHING

© 2015 Greenleaf Publishing Limited

Published by Greenleaf Publishing Limited
Aizlewood's Mill
Nursery Street
Sheffield S3 8GG
UK
www.greenleaf-publishing.com

Cover by Sadie Gornall-Jones
Photo by silvergull/ Shutterstock.com, depicting Antony Gormley's 'Another Place',
Crosby Beach

Printed and bound by Printondemand-worldwide.com, UK

British Library Cataloguing in Publication Data:
A catalogue record for this book is available from the British Library.

ISBN-13: 978-1-78353-173-8 [paperback]
ISBN-13: 978-1-78353-174-5 [hardback]
ISBN-13: 978-1-78353-171-4 [PDF ebook]
ISBN-13: 978-1-78353-172-1 [ePub ebook]

Let your life lightly dance on the edges of Time
Like a dew on the tip of a leaf
Rabindranath Tagore

All things hang like a drop of dew
Upon a blade of grass
W.B. Yeats

Contents

Acknowledgements

A book long in gestation and written on the road in bars, cafes and places all over the world over a few years makes for many people to thank. First among these is my long-suffering wife Louise. My ever-loving daughters Sophie and Cleo have suffered the slings and arrows of my outrageous good fortune. Then, in no particular order, are tips, challenges and sparks of vivid illuminesence from Mark Diesendorf, Mark Swilling, Georg Kell, Eve Anneke, Stephan Schaltegger, John van Breda, David Grayson, Renata Frolova, David Vidal, Sandra Waddock, Steve Waddell and GOLDEN's Large Systems Change research group, Jeremy Williams, Peter Lacy, Amina Aitsi-Selma, Nick Barter, Sally Russell, Jane Nelson, Paul Burton, Cate Mack, Richard White, Tim Smit, Jonathon Porritt, Sara Parkin, Crispin Tickell, Tim Flannery, Derick de Jongh, Alan Feest, David Pencheon, Clare Brass, Mohammed Wanous, Judy Ireton, David Murphy, Jem Bendell, Matt Gitsham, Simon Pickard, Mark Moody-Stuart, David Omand, Ruth Thomas, Mark Hudson, Richard White, Graham Carter, Karen Brindley,

Mari Kondo, Alan Hunter, and all the students and conference participants who have pointed out inconsistencies and deviations along the way. Thank you all. And, last but not least, the team at Greenleaf Publishing (as was), in particular my sub-editor and old friend Dean Bargh. Long may you ride.

First thoughts and preface

This is a book about change, about change that is happening now – what might be called rapid evolution. It is transitionary, necessary, nascent and ineluctable. It is a book about the past, the present and the future and it is about theory and practice. It contains evidence, anecdote, musings and passion. It is set in the second decade of the twenty-first century and has been written while I have been undergoing treatment for incurable cancer. Writing, and my good medical teams in Australia and the UK, have kept me alive, as has my absolute determination to treat this vicissitudinous deeply unfashionable lifestyle with positive energy. It's not warfare, or a battle, as it's often portrayed in the media, but a natural evolution. At the time of writing I'm still alive! It – cancer – is unwelcome when it visits, and, if one lives, it delivers a roller coaster life of highs and lows. On some days it's more akin to a big dipper. If this state of mind has affected my writing, then I'm happy to have had to look at life afresh and delighted with the resulting re-evaluation that miserablism is not the way.

Self-doubt, reflection and criticism are the two greatest assets for driven thinkers and avowedly public intellectuals. If your life is spent in prognostication, prophesising and pontificating (sometimes known as teaching), these things make your wisdom tenable, for, without the ability and candour to backtrack, nuance and evolve, we are nothing – ourselves, or as a species. Evolution, adaptation and learning are what make us progressive humans. So, too, love, laughter and learning make for an enjoyable life and make society possible.

In a life of enterprise, writing, public speaking, film making and teaching there is sometimes a gap between what I mean to do and say and what I am successful in doing and saying. The novelist Will Self expresses it well: 'to attempt to write something is always, I feel, to fail – the disjunction between my beautifully sonorous, accurate and painfully affecting mental content, and the leaden, halting sentences on the page always seems a dreadful falling short'.[1]

It is important to have an audience in mind when you write. For many years I worked for BBC TV and I often asked colleagues who their film was being made for: who did they have in mind? One very well-known producer with an award-winning international standing claimed he always made films not for a vast audience but for the auntie who had brought him up. Others would say that their test was a lover, a partner, a colleague or a man in their favourite pub. It was only afterwards that they considered a wider audience.

This book is written with the next generation in mind. For those in different continents and with varied dispositions: for

---

1 Will Self, 'Fail Better', *The Observer*, 22 June 2013: Review, 4.

the children of the world, in the hope that there might be a world for them to inhabit. They are the future. If I were to single out a specific place and space, this book is for the children of South Africa. I have been making annual visits to that country since 1998. On Nelson Mandela's 94th birthday, a year before he died, I was privileged to attend the morning assembly of all the children, aged 5 to 11, from Lynedoch primary school near Stellenbosch as they sang 'Happy Birthday Madiba'. And the caged bird sang with clarity, beauty and love.

In the days after Madiba died, Graça Machel and Winnie Mandela's quiet dignity saved the day at the rain-sodden memorial service. US President Barack Obama lifted the tone with the line that Mandela 'freed the prisoner *and* the jailer' and made links between the struggle against apartheid and the struggle for civil rights in the US. The same post-colonial struggle is going on around the world from Australia to the Middle East. Now it is an *economic* and *social* apartheid that the world faces, brought about by an ideological commitment to money as the arbiter of all good things.

This book is optimistic. I used to be a miserablist, but now I am reborn. As John Maynard Keynes said, 'there is no harm in being sometimes wrong – especially if one is promptly found out'. Well, it's taken me a whole lifetime. Winston Churchill similarly praised the art of trial and error: 'Criticism may not be agreeable, but it is necessary. It fulfils the same function as the human body; it calls attention to the development of an unhealthy state of things. If it is heeded in time, danger may be averted; if it is suppressed, a fatal distemper may develop.'

As you will read in this book, inspirations have come from re-reading, and in some cases reading for the first time, human and cosmological evolutionary theory and practice. In particular, I have been enveloped in the lives, among others, of Peter

Higgs and Charles Darwin, Rachel Carson and Beatrix Potter, William Golding and James Lovelock, Steven Pinker and Arnold Toynbee, Karl Marx and Adam Smith, Peter Drucker and Eric Hobsbawm, Julian Barnes and Richard Wilkinson, Amartya Sen and Noam Chomsky, Tony Judt and Jonathan Glover, Ian Morris and Pankaj Mishra, David Cannadine and Niall Ferguson, Colin Crouch and Thomas Piketty, William Shakespeare and Danny Dorling.

I make no apology for the title of this book having being inspired by Tony Judt and Timothy Snyder's magnificent book *Thinking the Twentieth Century* – except that they had the benefit of hindsight and I have the impediment of foresight.

This roll call of a varied bunch of cosmologists, evolutionary theorists, storytellers, management theorists, economists and historians evinces a transdisciplinary and truncated list of divergent approaches – so it will suit those people who agree with Albert Einstein that 'The fairest thing we can experience is the mysterious. It is the fundamental emotion which stands at the cradle of true art and true science. He who knows it not and can no longer wonder, no longer feel amazement, is as good as dead, a snuffed-out candle.'[2]

Fear, complacency and action

This book makes five simple points, although the arguments are anything but simple. Five systems changes are now taking place in the evolution of humanity. They are necessary and ineluctable, albeit random and not necessarily synchronistic.

2 Albert Einstein, *Autobiographical Notes* (Chicago: Open Court Publishing Company, 1979): 3-5.

Perhaps they are necessarily happening because they must, and because they would happen anyway given the propensity for survival that life forms have. The changes discussed in this book are all transitionary, nascent, ineluctable *and* necessary.

Our dilemma as a species is one of fear and complacency. A useful example is to be found in Shakespeare's *Othello*. At a production of the play at the National Theatre in London I was seriously motivated not to attend the second half, even though we all know how the play ends, such was the totally convincing easy evil of Rory Kinnear's Iago. (He later won an Olivier Award for his performance.) I wanted, probably like so many before, to leap on stage and stop Othello murdering his wife, Desdemona, for apparently having had an affair with Othello's best friend Cassio. This seems to me to be a parable on life: we know what might give us increased mortality, if not immortality, but are so driven by the moment that we fail to act now in order to save the future.

Many have commented on the seeming ease with which evil is allowed to grow in our midst; Hannah Arendt, commenting in 1963 on Adolf Eichmann's trial of the previous year, used the expression 'the banality of evil'. Eichmann was one of Hitler's lieutenants.

I felt the same watching Steve McQueen's *Twelve Years a Slave* in Brisbane, Australia. I felt I was part of the cruelty. I felt involved in every act of the evil by the bible-quoting slave owners and traders and I was with the victims at every step, singing every song, willing on every act of kindness. And yet, like the slaves in the film – and at the time – I was unable to act. I just sat as a member of the audience while the injustice played out in front of me. I wanted to scream. Like many others, by the end of the film I was weeping in shame and pain. There are First Peoples alive in Australia now, in the early twenty-first century, with living memories of Friday night lynchings of their people. As recently as the 1970s they had no voting rights and were cast as flora and fauna in the constitution. I want to scream. Like many others, I weep in shame and pain at this situation.

Being active in the fields of corporate responsibility and sustainability sometimes provokes the same sense of frustration. There is the pure thought and the good intention, the action and the inaction. The man who stood in front of the tanks in Tiananmen Square on 5th June 1989, whose picture has become synonymous with the Chinese Communist Party's image in the global public eye, was one such dramatic failure – or success. In a current parallel with the Chinese tanks, how much reportage is necessary to stop the fast-food monoliths that are causing so much obesity and illness and increased healthcare costs around the world? Or the banking industry that even since the 2008/9 crash operates as much to please itself as to service the needs of communities?

Like modern fast food, handguns in the wrong hands also kill: how much madness does it take to stop what seems a no-brainer? In 2012 Yoko Ono tweeted the statistic that since her husband John Lennon had been killed – shot dead on the street in New York outside the Dakota apartment building near Central Park on 8th December 1980 – 1,057,000 people had been killed by guns in the USA. The 15,000 re-tweeters of Ono's message included US President Barack Obama.

In 1964 my mother took me to St Paul's Cathedral in London to hear a man she said was 'very important and going to be more so'. He was, she said, 'a great moral leader' and she wanted me to hear him. I was eleven years old. We stood behind a pillar but by leaning sideways I could see the orator: Martin Luther King. He was on his way to Oslo to receive the Nobel Peace Prize; I cannot remember what he said on that day but I bless my mother for putting me in the presence of such a great leader. He died four years later on 4th April 1968 at the hands of a gun owner in Memphis, USA. It was not until January 2013 that President Obama inaugurated the first federally funded research on gun crime violence and declared gun crime 'a national health emergency'.

Sometimes it feels like a failure to be active: every day the world looks pretty much the same as the next day despite profound and well-intentioned efforts. On many days this is how building the sustainable enterprise society looks. It is said that all political lives end in failure, and I wonder if this is also true of good leaders. But they, unlike politicians, may not always be aware of their roles: that they are leaders. Good, as opposed to tyrannical or irresponsible, leaders may not know they are leaders until someone taps them on the shoulder and says 'you have led us up the hill so that we can see and claim the promised land'.

The personal problem is one of being too close to the subject, too mired in the muck of everyday action and reflection – of taking it too personally. But the personal is political. And politics can lead to action.

I have come to understand that environmental sustainability is *merely* a reiteration of the human dilemma, writ large and supported by today's knowledge. It is the ultimate test of our innocence to be told that the very thing that we need to survive is under threat, that the woman or man with whom we are in love is in fact dying before our eyes. Many a climate change scientist has told me that it is necessary to suffer cognitive dissonance when going to sleep at night, or when talking about the future to their grandchildren, such is the enormity of what we now know about the state of *planethome*.

I do not wish to confound or confront or disprove the many scientists that I have regular contact with when they tell me the apparent truth about climate change and the coming apocalypse. I do not *not* believe their science as far as I can understand it. But I do not believe that we are 'living in the end times' as Slavoj Žižek and others would have us believe.[3] I have become an optimist because, if evolution, adaptation and learning means that humanity has a short run, so be it. Ashes to ashes, dust to dust, stardust to stardust. We will have been a brilliant, marvellous miracle. So be it. Let it be. As the oldest religious text, the Vedas, say: the gods themselves are later than creation.

Climate change and conflict

Often, looking out across the valley, with scenes of green trees, red roses, distant hills, productive fields, swooping birds, calling gulls, buzzing bees and the smell of cut grass, I do not want to believe in this non-future, and so I won't. And I don't think this is what some psychologists will call denial on my part. It is because, when I take medium- and long-term views back over the history of the planet and our history, I am hopeful of an evolving reality. I don't even want to delve into the 'if we don't do this, then this is inevitable' discussion.

The question that has arisen in my general but informed discussions around the world and also with people who are deemed to be experts in their field, from various intellectual disciplines, is that the signs are good: that the science beyond and apart from the pure climate change science is good.

3 Slavoj Žižek, *Living in the End Times* (London: Verso, 2011).

The apocalypse is always with us because we think too much and it is easy for our minds to perceive of threats, real and imagined, and because we are part of nature. There is a sense in which sustainability is the child of the Second World War baby-boomer generation from Europe and North America for whom growing stability, growing economic wealth, increased liberty and participation, and lengthening lifespans have been the story of their lives. And I am one of these people, born into the destruction and chaos of 1950s England, growing up in the magnificent aspirations of the 1960s and '70s hippie generation who either went down the altruistic, collective path to social change or down the road to selfish individualism and neoliberalism. But both these paths have crossed and delivered their separate visions, and become entwined, forty and more years on.

I accept as read the science on climate change (but see Chapter 2: 'Rebalancing science and awe'), so this book is not about that subject; but it is about what we do, now that we know. Alternative subtitles for this book could be 'Now that we know what we know, what shall we do? What does this mean for the relationship between people and planet? What does it mean to be human in this century?'

I accept the overwhelming evidence that the carbon-based economy has to stop. This means significant changes to some staples of current life: changes to transport, heating, farming, chemicals, plastic, to be prosaic. The innovation, enterprise and learning involved in this change is one of the greatest challenges humans have ever faced and involves profound upheaval, dislocation and disruption on the one hand, but, on the other hand, liberation from the carbon obsession, and an initial rapid long-term upward investment and then a slower downward set of running costs, also over the long term. Like building a bridge that lasts for a hundred years, or a cathedral or temple that stands for thousands of years. We've done it before; we can do it again.

We are always searching for Utopia, but does the journey towards it have to be conflictual, or can it be a natural evolution? Were Marx, Darwin and Hobbes right in saying that that it has been fraught with conflict, or would I Ching's flow be more metaphoric, euphoric and natural?

Corporate responsibility and progress

Once upon a time I was deeply engaged in the corporate responsibility movement as a negotiator, an activist, a publisher and an educator. I was a fellow traveller in the UN Global Compact, SA8000, the Global Reporting Initiative, ISO 26000 and a whole host of other well-meaning multi-sector, multi-stakeholder initiatives. We were endeavouring to change business behaviour on the side of the angels, or so we thought. These were, and are, all good things, but I now realise that they missed the mark by a long way. In fact, it may be that engagement in this discourse and the flood of *voluntary* corporate responsibility initiatives has been the precursor to some bigger action where we begin to tackle more fundamental systems issues rather than tinkering at the edges.

The corporate responsibility movement has had several elements, all of them well-meaning and useful but fundamentally self-serving and self-absorbing and very rarely systems-changing.

There wasn't, and isn't, a single person on the proactive NGO and activist side who didn't have a progressive agenda, and if they were engaging actively their aim was, through talk, negotiation and compromise, to broker deals that would lead to a better version of capitalism. It was possible, we thought, for business to be kinder and more caring and to deliver through the invisible hand the sort of social contract envisaged by the post-WWII settlement and the development of the welfare state with the private and public sectors acknowledging their separate strengths and delivering together in a mixed economy. Sometimes the public sector needed adjustment, and sometimes the private sector showed its greed too much. But with checks and balances, in Europe and other parts of the advanced industrial democracies at least, a golden age from about 1945–1980 was reached and we had increased equality, growing longevity, universal healthcare, a good welfare safety net, full(ish) employment and growing material prosperity, all within an increase in flourishing democracies.

Even in the second decade of the twenty-first century, Europe scores well on almost every indicator of civilisation: longevity, universal healthcare provision, street safety, gender equality, low corruption, income equality, peacefulness, democracy, gun control, and the absence of capital punishment.[4] We had seen this in Europe, Scandinavia, Canada and in other parts of the world like Japan and Australia, so why not universally and globally?

One of the recent learnings for me, and a pleasant surprise, is that overall, in aggregate, standing back, it worked. Seven and more decades on from the end of WWII, the world, the whole world and not just Europe and parts of North America,

---

4 These are figures from a wide range of global research bodies including the CIA, the World Economic Forum, Transparency International, the World Health Organisation and the UN. (I list them as examples of the wealth of international data that helps us understand the new international political economy.)

Australasia and Japan, is a better, more peaceful place than it has ever been. It is possible, looking at the statistics ranging from infant mortality to education to peacefulness to longevity, to show that human progress has flourished and that as a race we can be proud of our achievements. We have done well despite the naysayers, doom-mongers and apocalypse merchants.

Why, then, is a radical transition necessary if all is well with our world? The answer is that the model that we now have, which has worked relatively well, will no longer work in the future. As an intelligent race we know this, and, having foresight, we must understand that out short-lived success can only be continued if we acknowledge how we reached this place, and understand what it means to be human in this century, and acknowledge the changes that are now necessary.

Robins Orchard, Goodshelter,
South Hams, Devon, England
September 2014

Introduction

It is the second decade of the twenty-first century, as measured by the Western world, and we are where we are. A starting point for this book, which is subtitled 'The *New* Political Economy', is a statement from a UN advisory group. In 2012 the United Nations Secretary-General's High-Level Panel on Global Sustainability called for both an intellectual transdisciplinary and cross-sectoral approach to sustainable development by calling for a 'new political economy'. Sustainable development is a wide term and encompasses more than an interest in environment and economics.

> For too long, economists, social scientists and social activists and environmental scientists have talked past each other – almost speaking different languages, or at least different dialects. The time has come to unify the disciplines, to develop a common language for sustainable development that transcends the warring camps; in other words, to bring the sustainable development paradigm into mainstream economics ... That is why the Panel

> argues that the international community needs
> what some have called 'a new political economy'
> for sustainable development.[1]

A lifetime spent criss-crossing the planet speaking, researching and writing, making films, advising governments, corporations and the United Nations – and also often just hanging out
watching the world go by – has not taught me about the differences between us, although there are some and they are often
pointed and sharp, but about what binds us together. I have
learnt about our commonality and the journey we are all on. I
have learnt about evolution, adaptation and learning.

I have learnt that the things that fundamentally change the
world are ideas, institutions and technologies. In the modern
world these are as likely to be spread by corporate interests as
any other vehicle. Corporations have become, at the moment,
the *modus operandi* – a common way of making things happen, but not the only way. Social media may be the way many
people – but not all – consume their day; it is thought of as
all-consuming and liberating, but it is possible to wonder if
it is just a medium that is now dominated by profit-making
interests. It is a technology that connects us globally and gives
us access to ideas, but which also subverts us into increased
consumption. We live in an era of mass, cheap, easily accessible
technology and ideas. Everything is marketised, commoditised
and objectified, including how to save the world *and* how to
destroy the Earth.

Every time has its issues. Sixteenth-century Europe, for
instance, wanted a solution to the plagues that ravaged whole

1 United Nations Secretary-General's High-Level Panel on Global
Sustainability, *Resilient People, Resilient Planet: A Future Worth
Choosing* (New York: United Nations, 2012): Overview, 5.

communities (as is happening now in parts of Africa and Asia), the result of which was that at the end of William Shakespeare's life the population of Europe was half the size it was when he was born. At that time death in childbirth was so common for women and babies, as was death generally, that Shakespeare makes few references to the plague in his plays.

In 1850 the London population grew to 1 million people and the city needed a transport solution. The enlightened decision was made to start building what came to be known as the Underground or the Tube, with the first train running on the Metropolitan Line in 1863. Victorian Britain also saw the introduction of sewerage systems to take the shit out of the streets, albeit initially simply dumping it downstream in the River Thames.

Compulsory conscription in the UK in 1914 was a wake-up call for healthcare systems that could provide healthy men to feed both the trenches and the factories, which led, thirty years later – after the Second World War – to the world's first universally free-at-the-point-of-delivery healthcare system with the birth of the UK's National Health Service in 1948.

And on . . . William Anders took the first picture of the Earth from the Moon in 1968, the Berlin Wall finally fell in 1989, the white population of South Africa finally ceded power to democracy in 1994, the first barcode was used in 1973, Tim Berners-Lee and colleagues invented the World Wide Web in (only) 1989, the US started using drones to bomb civilians in 2004, Dolly the sheep was 'born' on July 5th 1996 (and died in 2003) . . .

The five necessary, nascent and ineluctable systems changes

The five systems changes discussed in this book involve the onward march of globality and Earth systems connectedness, and humanity learning to live within its planetary limits. They are nascent systems changes that involve shifts in global consciousness. This is not revolution: it is evolution, adaptation and learning. Revolutions are rarely complete overturnings; rather, viewed from a later time and with a longer perspective, they look like perturbations in a flowing river, or inevitabilities in the passage of time.

The five systems changes that this book claims to be ineluctable are not necessarily discrete, and this book does not claim one over another as the main field of progress. They are as interconnected as they are subsets of each other.

Given that one of the recurring themes in the history of humanity is fear of 'the other' and the setting of one group against another, often leading to war, this book makes the point that we – humanity – are on the same trajectory each and every one, one and all. Indeed, that which divides us also unites us because the idea of division is common to all nations, tribes, groups and communities. David Cannadine in *The Undivided Past* points out that identity has been a way of emphasising differences between groups and that being different is one of the essences of what it means to be human; yet, paradoxically, the fact that we share this characteristic unites us.[2] This conflict identity tends to be reinforced by our mythologies, collective memories and religions. But, standing back and extending our

2 David Cannadine, *The Undivided Past: History Beyond Our Differences* (London: Allen Lane, 2013).

timeline perspective, we see that life on Earth, which has been short, brutish and often conflictual, is now becoming something different. We are in the midst of an immense, rapid and irreversible shift in consciousness and perception which will leave us facing outwards again to the stars.

Individual lives will always be a struggle, full of triumph and disaster. That is the nature of life on planet Earth for all living material, climbing as we do out of the primordial sludge every day with our reptilian brains leading the way as we drink, eat, swallow, fart, fuck our way to a place where we can sit and think for a moment, to a place where we can, if we are lucky, be conscious in the fullest sense – and look over the fertile valley below. At this point, in the twenty-first century, some 11,700 years after the last ice age and some 60,000 years after humankind journeyed slowly out of its origins in Africa,[3] 400,000 years after something human-like first walked the Earth,[4] and about 4.54 billion years since some of the stardust settled to

3 Or did this occur much earlier? See Hugo Reyes-Centenoa, Silvia Ghirottob, Florent Détroitc, Dominique Grimaud-Hervéc, Guido Barbujanib and Katerina Harvati, 'Genomic and cranial phenotype data support multiple modern human dispersals from Africa and a southern route into Asia', *Proceedings of the National Academy of Sciences of the United States of America* 111.20 (2014); www.pnas.org/content/111/20/7248.

4 The Homo genus first appeared about 2.4 million years ago. Four hundred thousand years ago is when Homo erectus started to increase in skull size on its way to becoming Homo sapiens. This, I would note, is an evolving field with new discoveries on almost a weekly basis. As I am not an expert in this field, but, as this book says, a transdisciplinarian, I am subject to the varying accounts which provide a wonderful debate on the inexactitudes of evolutionary theory; but this is what makes knowledge discovery so much fun.

form this planet, we know enough to understand that we are conscious and that we are both victims of our wilfulness and at the same time cast adrift in space. It is possible, in other words, to believe in science, free will, predestination and awe at the same time, and in the same breath of life. I have quoted Albert Einstein before and I repeat it here: 'The fairest thing we can experience is the mysterious. It is the fundamental emotion which stands at the cradle of true art and true science. He who knows it not and can no longer wonder, no longer feel amazement, is as good as dead, a snuffed-out candle.'[5]

Individual lives matter, and one of the moral purposes of life is to extend sympathy and empathise with our fellow human beings. But it is the collective in the grand sweep of history that is most interesting to study; for one individual is merely a part of a greater whole, part human, part Earthly, part cosmic.

There are two issues at the heart of this book. First, how do we see the world now? In other words, what does it mean to be human now that we know what we know? Second, how are we organised as humans in our various groupings and how do these groupings, mobs, or organisations, reflect where we have travelled to thus far? Who are we and how do we know each other?

The 2012 UN report *Resilient People, Resilient Planet: A Future Worth Choosing* called for a 'new political economy', but sustainable development is not the only reason for the five issues discussed in this book.

5 Einstein, *Autobiographical Notes*: 3-5.

There are five reasons why we need a new political economy

The first reason relates to sustainable development and its con-comitant, globality and Earth awareness, where for the first time we see and feel the world as one entity in our minds and hearts. This is globality and Earth awareness: the idea of one shared space. This involves a better understanding of our history and the history of the planet, and most fundamentally understanding our biological, physical and neural connectivity on this one small place in space called planet Earth. When we can see our infinitesimability in space we will feel our vulnerability together – again.

The second is concerned with the highest level of evolution – the evolution of knowledge – and in this case the evolution of the balance between what we think we know and what we feel, intuit and discuss. We have come to a critical juncture in which awe and wonder have been marginalised by science, modernity, technology, consumerism and neoliberal economics. We need to look again at the balance of knowing and not knowing, of rebalancing science and awe. The distinction between science and scepticism has always been a fine line, sometimes connected and often very disconnected. New knowledge has always challenged old nostrums and ways of doing things, and new technologies arising from new knowledge have led some groups of people to overpower other groups and trample on their evolution. The balance between what is obvious through learning and what is sacred through belief, ritual and religion is as treacherous as the balance between markets and democracy.

Third, the rise of empathy and social, perhaps global, cohesion is a natural progression from the first and second systems changes outlined here. I call this nurturing spirit the rise of the feminisation of decision-making and governance as it is a fundamental recognition that the rise and success of the human race is due as much to empathy, sociability, sharing and group work as it is to competition, aggression and masculinity. We are in the process of rebalancing the yin and the yang. Despite the continuous display of graphic violence on our minds (and on the minds of children), the world has been getting more peaceful since 1945. This fact is accompanied by less use of violence and physical force than in any previous period of human history. Also the mechanisation of much industrial, building and manufacturing activity has seen traditional masculinity threatened and a new breed of man emerging: the feminised man – a gentle, caring, sharing, nurturing fellow as much at home pushing a buggy as he is wearing moisturiser. If the industrial revolution was a shift from muscle to machine, the current information age is a shift from the analogue to the digital with similar disruptive mental shifts occurring.

The fourth systems change concerns the way we organise ourselves as humans, based, as we are – at the moment – on planet Earth. The way we organise our organisations and our institutions is inexorably changing. Our institutions and organisations reflect who we think we are and how we have been up to now, but their inbuilt inertia now acts to prevent us moving on. If we do not accept that our organising principles may not be harmonious with what we now know about the planet and ourselves, we will fail to make the necessary transition. For these institutions and organisations are pre-set to carry on regardless and we are but blind agents in their Titanic-like travel. It will not be possible to seize control of the institutional wheelhouse without mass public support, for why would the current beneficiaries want to stop the juggernauts that have brought so much success so far.

Fifth, evolutionary success and human survival depends on our ability to learn, on our learning adaptability and our ability to adapt through learning. The way we learn, and our approach to education – the two should become synonymous – will determine our chances of survival. We deny our evolutionary history at our peril. We may be adaptive and fast learners but we are still animals and raising each and every one of us out of the swamp of reptilian thought and action requires continuous effort and eternal vigilance, to adapt a well-known line about the price of freedom.[6]

These five changes are necessary and are happening anyway, even if the forces of inertia and conservatism seek to put a brake on them. Just as there is an increase in the frequency of apparently random weather extremes in the form of hurricanes, cyclones, droughts and floods, so too the post-1945 social consensus is over. The social welfare reforms coupled to massive innovations in productivity over the last sixty years that led to the greatest redistribution of wealth and improvement in most people's lives may be coming to an end as elites no longer necessarily need so many people to labour in their factories, sweatshops and fields to deliver the 1% of the world's financial wealth. What is referred to as the Long Peace may be over and just as 'Pax Britannica' led to 'Pax Americana' we are now entering a period of 'Pax Interdependence' (just so long as we can keep a lone political madman with a nuclear device from blowing us all away).

'You may say I'm a dreamer' John Lennon sang, and former Czech Republic President Václav Havel similarly echoed the song 'Imagine' when he wrote: 'Some say I'm a naïve dreamer

6 'The price of freedom [or liberty] is eternal vigilance' is variously attributed to Thomas Jefferson, Wendell Phillips, Thomas Paine, Abraham Lincoln, Leonard H. Courtney and many others.

who is always trying to combine the incompatible: politics and morality'. Havel refers to Marxist revolutionary philosophy which claims to have 'scientifically comprehended the entire history of the world'. 'The idea that the world might actually be changed by the force of truth, the power of the truthful word, the strength of a free spirit, conscience, and responsi-bility – with no guns, no lust for power, no political wheel-ing and dealing – was quite beyond the horizon of [Marx's] understanding.'[7] And so it is that much of what is happen-ing now is ineluctable, nascent and transitionary. Some of the forces we think of as conflictual have in reality, with a longer-term perspective, an inevitability.

The myth of sustainability

Sustainability is the Western myth of eternal life and the tran-scendence of nature. I feel happier thinking about adaptation, resilience, impermanence, respect – and harmony. My constitu-ent parts have been here forever and will be when I leave; it is my infernal mind and ego that will not rest and think(s) it should be eternal. As soon as we stop talking about sustainable development and sustainability and remember who we are and where we are, we will feel happier to know that we are adap-tive, learning, sharing, living and dying beings with an innate capacity for love, learning, awe and having fun. Love, laugh-ter and learning are what make us human. As Mark Twain is alleged to have said, 'I do not fear death. I had been dead for

7 Václav Havel, *Summer Meditations* (London: Vintage Books, 1992): 5.

billions and billions of years before I was born, and had not suffered the slightest inconvenience from it.'

The greatest practical and political challenges for immediate attention are: understanding our relationship to the Earth's lithosphere and particularly the carbon cycle; developing global citizenship allied to local living; and changing the social systems and institutions that run our lives, from finance and banking to multinational corporations and government.

This is not so difficult and the change is already happening even if we cannot always see it. Climate change is with us; new models of social, mutual and networked business are evolving; a global neural revolution is under way; and the reptilian and ugly masculinity is slowly giving way at the macro level to the nuanced, the complex and the feminine.

The inspirations for this book

Those that have inspired me, and countless others who are worth re-reading, include Rachel Carson, whose ground-breaking book *Silent Spring* begins: 'There was once a town in the heart of America where all life seemed to live in harmony with its surroundings.' Carson has been compared to Charles Darwin, another breaker of models, who inspired Carson in his *On the Origin of Species*: 'We behold the face of nature bright with gladness, we often see superabundance of food; we do not see, or we forget, that the birds which are idly singing round us mostly live on insects or seeds, and are thus constantly destroying life.'

Carson was born almost exactly one hundred years after Darwin and followed the same intellectual lineage: both were brilliant, disciplined natural scientists *and* social reformers.

Both changed their views on life and politics because of a conversion brought about by the evidence that nature and science presented to them in their fieldwork. It would be good to see the return of the polymath and the natural philosopher.

Born over 80 years before Darwin, Adam Smith (1723–1790) and James Hutton (1726–1797) have, through their work, had as much impact as Darwin and Carson on the way we live and the way the social world works. Carson and Darwin have been compared to James Lovelock, and no less controversially either. Moving to the twentieth century, and on into the twenty-first, I want to link these figures with a number of the most enlightened thinkers on management, business and economics. One of these, Peter Drucker, died aged 95 in 2005, having published his first book *The End of Economic Man in 1939* and his last, *Management Challenges for the 21st Century*, in 1999. He stressed that capitalism and business were social constructs which should serve society, and not the reverse.

In the twenty-first century we need these kinds of minds more than ever, but we need to find the time to read them. This book reaches back to these, and other, thinkers and writers in order to see where Robert Frost's 'road not taken' might lead this century. It is profoundly optimistic, not because I want to be contrarian against all the pessimists such as Slavoj Žižek, Martin Rees and others, but because I want to show that a profound belief and relief in the unknown, and not-knowingness is the best future we have.

In *The Necessary Transition*, a book of essays published in 2013, I said in the Introduction: 'That we are in the midst of a major transition in the history of humanity there is no doubt, but you can choose your transition point.'[8] I listed the issues of

---

8 Malcolm McIntosh (ed.), *The Necessary Transition: The Journey towards the Sustainable Enterprise Economy* (Sheffield, UK: Greenleaf Publishing, 2013): 1.

climate change, social justice, population and finance systems as major transition points. I argued for

> the transition that is necessary in order to move locally and globally to a socially just sustainable enterprise economy.[9] Life on Earth for humanity is changing and our ecosystems are at a point of great change, and there is much to be learnt from previous disruptions. The key words are 'learning', 'adaptation' and 'transformation'.[10]

This book continues with these ideas. Gregory Bateson said in *Steps to an Ecology of Mind* in 1972: 'We would do well to hold back our eagerness to control the world which we so imperfectly understand . . . rather, our studies could be inspired by a more ancient, but today less honoured, motive: a curiosity about the world of which we are part. The rewards of such work are not power, but beauty.'[11]

We live in an era of fear, particularly in the US, and intolerance within and between some religious, ethnic, national and tribal groups. We have adopted consumerism and technology as ends in themselves. And we have an almost fanatical attraction to the blind pursuit of growth and financial profit. Classical economics has morphed into the neoliberal model where everything is financialised. We are wedded to a particular model of economics that enslaves humanity and rapes the

---

9 For an understanding of the starting points for a sustainable enterprise economy, please see Sandra Waddock and Malcolm McIntosh, *SEE Change: Making the Transition to a Sustainable Enterprise Economy* (Sheffield, UK: Greenleaf Publishing, 2012).

10 McIntosh, *The Necessary Transition*: 1.

11 Gregory Bateson, *Steps to an Ecology of Mind: Collected Essays in Anthropology, Psychiatry, Evolution, and Epistemology* (Chicago: University of Chicago Press, 1972): 269.

Earth, destroying that which sustains us. It is not economics per se that is wrong, for economics is merely an area of study, learning and development, but the adherence to a *particular* model of neoliberal economics that is preached by priests (and a few priestesses) as being rational, truthful, ultimate, absolute and 'the way'. Rather than being seen as an exploration with ragged edges, the current economic model occupies the high ground of scientific rationality and morality – it has the feel of religious and irrational fervour. And what an irony: its apostles claim that the market, if allowed to flow freely, is rational and self-balancing and built on autopoiesis. The priests claim that the market is rational, moral and socially good. Can autopoiesis be rational, or is it intuitive?

The current economic model defies enlightenment thinking which emphasises tolerance, unknowns, exploration, balances, respect for other ideas, and awe in art and science. But we live in a world of instant answers, gratification and apparent rationality. John Kay, an economic contrarian, says that 'this addiction to the idea that every problem has an answer, even and especially if that answer may be difficult to find, meets a deeply held human need'. This is the asocial artificial world of computer games, with their linear modelling. 'Many economists are similarly asocial [and] it is probably no accident that economics is by far the most male of the social sciences.'[12] But more of this theme in Chapter 3.

The history of humanity is about adaptation to changed conditions and about facing a future that builds on success, while recognising that success has come about through learning. The difference this century is that, whereas in the past time

12 John Kay, 'Circular Thinking: Models that offer universal descriptions of the world have led economists to repeat their mistakes', *RSA Journal* 4 (2013): 13.

moved at a glacial pace – socially and relatively speaking – now it thunders along like a river in full flood. Whereas it is not so long ago that most people understood that their children would have much the same lives as themselves, now we know that our children's future will be very different from our own. It is not that we can or should wish to slow down change, but it is so important that we do not forget where we came from and the baggage we carry.

The industrialisation phase of human development is only just over two hundred years old. A generation is normally thought of as about 25 years, so the industrial revolution is just ten generations old, with enough time to forget. But, when my grandmother died at the age of 97 towards the end of the last century, she had lived through half of this human epoch, and, as she was fond of telling us, she had seen horses become cars, birds become planes, newspapers become television news, information become instant, and world wars become a distant memory in the second half of the century. She had lived through two world wars, collected horse dung on Barnet Hill, taken in Jewish refugees and been proud to spend nearly forty years working in the UK's National Health Service. The point of this anecdote is to say that it is possible to think of the birth of the industrial revolution being only three generations ago. She was fond of saying that the future had speeded up, which rather than being a sign of old age, was recognition that in the fields of communications technology, weaponry and transport she had seen a revolution within a revolution.

It is commonplace to stand before a class of bright-eyed students at universities around the world and explain that the instant access of information, which is now so accepted as the status quo, was once a revolutionary idea, a twinkle in the eye of Tim Berners-Lee and others. Things have speeded up so much that it appears that revolutions now happen in an instant. But I want to ask: is it not the case that the fundamentals have not changed, and the foundations of our lives today were laid down millions of years ago, however much it may appear that every generation thinks it has invented sex, freedom and the future?

If we can learn to live peaceably and sustainably within planetary limits, this century will be a turning point in the history of humanity, just as the industrial revolution in the mid eighteenth century was in its time.

The necessary transition now under way everywhere in the world is for some a peaceful, even joyful happening, while for others it is being forced upon them and it is a time of chaos and destruction. The same was true with the industrial revolution in the late eighteenth and early nineteenth centuries, first in Britain and then Germany, closely followed by France, the remainder of Europe and then the United States of America. At its heart was the application of science, the development of technology, the mass exploitation of the Earth's lithosphere and the end of muscle power, along with the eruption of a new organisational model of capitalism. This has got us to where we are now: on the verge of collapse or blossom. I believe the latter is what will happen, albeit with similar cataclysmic side effects. But humanity has always had a bumpy ride, and the idea of apocalypse, real or imagined, has always been part of human existence. Indeed, many would say that a fear of uncertainty is what drives humans on, and is the font of all religions, science and aspiration.

So it is that the writers I have chosen to include in this book are representative of fundamental shifts in thinking about the relationship between people and planet, but only over the last few hundred years. It is through their thinking that we can see more clearly how we might think now, partly because their thinking pervades much of what happens to us on a day-to-day basis. But I will also point out that their thoughts would be more useful if they were not misrepresented and if the fullness of their wisdom was considered more carefully.

Writing this book

I began writing this book in 2012 and in that year a number of international events occurred with global implications. A sustainable development conference took place in Rio de Janeiro in Brazil. Rio was to host the FIFA World Cup in 2014 and the Olympic Games in 2016. The 2012 conference was called Rio+20 and followed on from the second world conference on the environment held in the same city in 1992, the first world conference on people and environment having taken place in Stockholm as recently as 1972.

In August 2012 the Olympic Games were held in London. In the previous year the Occupy Wall Street Movement had led to 600 occupations of city centres around the world in a celebration of the right to public protest, free thinking and democratic action.

These events are linked. A global picture is painted by means of international actions and global citizenships. And all the time I want to ask: what is the truth, and whose is it? With these questions in mind, I intend to address the largest and most important, and to some the most exciting, issues of our current century. And I suppose there are two paradoxes about the history of our 13.82-billion-year-old universe and the history of humanity, which reaches back millions of years. We forget our evolutionary past at our peril.

Paradox one is that we should be hopeful about the future, because there is much that is interesting, exciting and positive about uncertainty, especially as we are on the edge of a whole new world in every sense. The future was never Utopian, despite the fact that hope springs eternal, but, at the edge of the Anthropocene, [13] on the verge of the complete known and the complete unknown (another paradox), what we do know is that life on Earth for humans (and all flora and fauna) can never be as it was. Whereas for our recent ancestors only a few generations ago one childhood rolled into another, this time one childhood looks and feels very different from the last. But we must not forget our evolutionary past: we will always have to sleep, eat, drink and exercise but not necessarily fuck, fight and forget. As our brains morph with machines, we may know less, but think we actually know more.

Paradox two is that we now need to understand and cope with both simplicity and complexity at the same time as they are two sides of the same leaf, one exposed to the sun the other soaking up the nutrients. Just as we have belatedly come to the realisation that the climate is a complex system, so too are we slowly understanding that many of our self-created social systems are complex and not subject to mechanical or linear control. We need more nudge and meditation *and* also major command-and-control exercises. Our social systems may be out of control, and we must wrest back control if they are not to consume and control us. We should not be afraid of complexity, even as we sometimes long for simplicity.

Humanity's brief flirtation with life on Earth (or 'brief sojourn' as Einstein called it) is coming to an end and changing

---

13 Anthropocene: coined by Eugene Stoermer in the late 1980s and since adopted by many Earth scientists to denote the idea that human activity has led to a new geological age for Earth.

dramatically. 'It's life, but not as we know it' as the line in *Star Trek*, the TV series, used to say. All the signs – for humanity – are hopeful for the future, but with different lifestyles, new organisational and business models and institutions, and with an eye to life away from Earth, and with an awareness that our understanding of life is radically changing from one generation to another. The Anthropocene is leading to the age of interdependence – the planetary age – and onward to the cosmological age – or, the real space age. The realisation is slow and the forces of reaction, conservatism and inertia will hold us back, but, as Gro Harlem Brundtland said in 2012, prior to the Rio+20 Earth Summit in Rio de Janeiro, 'our generation is the first to understand the risks facing humanity'.[14]

Despite rejecting his negativity, I accept Slavoj Žižek's analysis of three threats: ecological breakdown, humans being manipulatable through biogenetics, and the digital control of our lives.[15] I would add a further issue, which is our growing inability to stop and think and find balance in our lives between what we know and don't know, and between doing, being and having. Having, or at least frenetic over-consumption, may be on the way out, and a more collaborative economy arising. As style guru Malcolm McLaren, who was instrumental in founding the punk movement in the late 1970s and '80s, said, 'we are at the end of the culture of desires; we may be going back to a culture of necessity'.[16] He links Karl Marx's creation and destruction of capital and Joseph Schumpeter's creative destruction in capitalism with punk: 'the bankers may have been the

---

14 Gro Harlem Brundtland, 'Earth Agonistes', *International Herald Tribune*, 19 June 2012: 8.
15 Žižek, *Living in the End Times*: 327.
16 Malcolm McLaren, 'This Much I Know', *Observer Magazine*, 16 November 2008: 10.

biggest punks of them all; they were making punk investments' which would necessarily implode. But have we learnt anything from the 2008/9 global credit crash, and have we yet instituted mechanisms and controls on our global financial systems to ensure that a repeat doesn't happen?

A further threat may therefore be added to those outlined here. The world is awash with systems that we have created but cannot control – viruses that have escaped. The mechanised and digitised global financial system may be as dangerous as the madman with the bomb. In other words, the organisations and institutions we have created through our masculine world dominated by competition, risk, enterprise and greed may eat us all. Goldman Sachs or Coca-Cola may be as out of control as the plagues were in European urban centres from 1400 onwards. While such global behemoths are obviously an enormous threat, I am optimistic and think that the 99% will find a way to tame the 1%, and that, as singer-songwriter Billy Bragg says, 'the big issue is going to be accountability rather than socialism: it's not about ideology any more, it's practical.'[17] I am also with fertility scientist Robert Winston when he says: 'I'm an optimist . . . human society is improving . . . would you rather live in 1913 or 2013?'[18] The answer may depend on where you live, Robert, but I get your drift.

The counterpoint to these three affluent western, northern European white men in their later lives – Winston, Bragg and McLaren – is that for those for whom life is not so mellifluent – those whose future, and that of their offspring, is shaking of the shackles of post-colonial Pax Britannica and Pax

---

17 Hester Lacey, 'A Walk with the FT: The Golden Cap Route', *Financial Times*, 5 June 2012; on.ft.com/1wcQgDE.

18 Robert Winston, 'The New Statesman Centenary Questionnaire', *New Statesman*, 1–7 November 2013: 70.

Americana – cannot come soon enough. The Indian historian Pankaj Mishra talks about the coming of the real cosmopolitan era when post-imperial pomp has been buried and the current pioneering rapacious model of capitalism has been transcended by a nurturing, collaborative economy based on enterprise, creativity and risk that arises from developing new strategies for mutuality, protection, resilience and human wealth creation. But more of thinkers from the east later in this book, but not without another word from Pankaj Mishra who says that most history is 'a narcissistic history . . . obsessed with western ideals, achievement, failures and challenges'.[19]

We create our own history but we must also build on our shared understanding of history to create a future based on a sense of one shared planet; on rebalancing what we know and we wonder at; on recognising that we can live peaceably as a global community; on reorganising around these principles; and on working on the nexus between evolution, adaptation and learning.

Human history has been based on evolution, adaptation and learning but there is a limit to how fast we can adapt physically, and some would say mentally. In reaching back into the past in the search for answers and by scanning the horizon for some sign of a way out of our current predicaments, many of the writers quoted in this book would beg us to see with different eyes. It is only with renewed vision and a different way of looking that we can possibly envision a future. One way is to allow us more time to wonder in a world of crazy exhortations to 'decide here and now on this flimsy information'. Another is to let our intuitive, feminine side blossom: to rebalance the yin and the yang – to think, feel and see harmony. But an even

19 Pankaj Mishra, 'A Righteous Nostalgia', *The Guardian*, 28 July 2012: Review, 2.

more powerful way of seeing the world is to know that it is the energy between things that makes the connections. As Fritjof Capra says:

> Systems thinking is relevant to all professions and academic disciplines that deal with life in one way or another – with living organisms, social systems, or ecosystems. Systems thinking is inherently multidisciplinary . . . The language of systems thinking came out of that crisis scientists confronted in the 1920s. Ever since Descartes, they had been searching for the smallest particle – from organisms to cells to molecules to quarks. But when they thought they had found the fundamental constituents of matter, they suddenly realized there are no fundamental constituents. It is all a web of connections and interrelations. Systems thinking thus helps us to understand how all the problems we confront are interconnected. There are no isolated solutions. We need interconnected solutions.[20]

This interconnectedness is crucial. That the five key issues addressed in this book are all connected should be obvious. To have them considered, and written about, together is less common.

---

20 Interview with Fritjof Capra, 'Systems Thinking and System Change: A Great Transition Initiative Interview', August 2014.

1

Rescuing globality

Astronaut Neil Armstrong, looking back at Earth from the Moon in 1968, said, 'I put up my thumb and shut one eye, and my thumb blotted out the planet Earth. I didn't feel like a giant. I felt very, very small.' Standing on Earth, make a small hole in the sky with your thumb and forefinger and hold it up to a dark patch in the night where there are no visible stars. But with a large enough telescope and a long enough exposure you could discern perhaps 100,000 galaxies each containing billions of stars. Since supernovae explode once per hundred years per galaxy, with 100,000 galaxies in view you should expect to see, on average, about three stars explode on any given night. Before industrialisation and night sky pollution, experiencing the connection of seeing the cosmos in glorious detail was commonplace for all humans.

For this chapter I have used the term 'globality' because it needs rescuing from those who have taken it to imply the end point of economic globalisation. This was Francis Fukuyama's mistake in 1992 when he said that neoliberalism equalled the end of history. Why does everything have to be seen through the lens of economics and financialisation? The answer is: it doesn't; and when I talk about globality I mean the sense of one shared space. In the 1960s the image of Spaceship Earth became common through the work of Kenneth Boulding and Barbara Ward.[1] I have previously called Earth *planethome*.[2]

It is also necessary to distinguish between globalisation, globalism and globality. I see these as separate but connected and interlinked phenomena. Globalisation and globalism are subsets of a growing sense of Earth awareness or globality.

The current form of twentieth- and twenty-first-century globalisation is an economic and political process convened by neoliberalists under the banner of market freedom and political tolerance for neoliberalism. Its essence is consumption and its vehicles are limited-liability companies; distanced investment and management; a firm belief that markets are the ultimate information system; that markets are rational; and that we are each and all of us rational decision-makers. Central to this fundamentalism is the nostrum that planning is per se, especially if it's public, a bad thing, and that public management is always inefficient. The evidence does not support this last fundamental tenet of neoliberalism.

Globalism currently runs parallel to globalisation but is slightly more benign in that it says that ideas can be non-economic. Globalism is the spread of ideas on a global basis whether they be the proselytising of Christianity or Islam, the

1 Barbara Ward, *Spaceship Earth* (New York: Columbia University Press, 1966).
2 Malcolm McIntosh, 'PlanetHome', in Rupesh A. Shah, David F. Murphy and Malcolm McIntosh (eds.), *Something To Believe In: Creating Trust and Hope in Organisations: Stories of Transparency, Accountability and Governance* (Sheffield, UK Greenleaf Publishing, 2003): 24-29.

Occupy movement, the United Nations, FIFA's World Cup or Nike's slash. The point about globalism, as a subset of globality, is that the spread of simple but affective ideas is as important as grand narratives.

Globality and Earth awareness is a change of consciousness from the political and economic frontier-building process of globalisation. This recaptured understanding of globality leads on from an understanding of the Anthropocene, and is connected to the coming cosmological or planetary age. Globality is not the end point of economic globalisation, as globalisation is bound to fail as it devours all in its way. The frontier economy will eat itself as it destroys its host.

Globality is simply an emotional, spiritual, aesthetic sense of the globe: that we share one liveable space, one planet, one home, planethome. Earth. If we do not grow this sense of globality, and if this sense is not built into our decision-making and governance structures, we will not survive as a species; for the forces of destruction, consumerism and resource depletion will meet themselves coming over the hill and in our end we will truly know our beginning.

The world is at a confused point as it moves from tribalism, nationalism and misogyny to emergent forms of global governance that are founded on a shared territory and not on territories stolen, fought for or devised. Many of the world's national boundaries were arbitrarily formed by European powers during the great period of colonisation and empire from 1750–1950. Because of this often arbitrary nation building, it is no surprise that most people when asked 'where do you come from?' respond with their national identity. But this is changing, as city-states become more powerful and natural geographical regions become more dominant. Paradoxically, the fact that nation-states rule is a source of stability and yet a scourge of the global governance debate: it is an accident of history rather than necessarily a sensible way to proceed. One of the issues, discussed later, that has emerged from the Occupy movement activists was that of identity: 'who are we (am I) in a globalised economy?' Perhaps encapsulating the dilemma for the new cosmopolitanism, the Canadian novelist Margaret Atwood said, 'you may be born somewhere, and you may die somewhere, but this doesn't necessarily define your identity'.[3]

Just look at the map of Africa, the Middle East or Australia and wonder at the very straight lines that cut through natural barriers such as rivers and mountain ranges and through bio-communities and social networks. Of course, these not-so-ancient organising systems, nation-states, are how we officially compartmentalise the world, but they are no longer the way the world is necessarily managed or the way many people now see themselves – or the way forward. The conservative force in the argument is that, at present, we have no other way of convening global, or dare I say 'international', meetings. Increasingly complex urban environments, or cities, meet to discuss governance with global corporations and realign the world around supply chains, consumers, markets and population density. This is the historian Arnold Toynbee in 1934: 'The spirit of nationality is a sour ferment of the new wine of democracy in old tribal bottles.'[4] Toynbee may not have been correct in equating nationalism to tribalism but he was correct in identifying nationalism as a *form* of tribalism, and danger-

3 Margaret Atwood, *Survival: A Thematic Guide to Canadian Literature* (Toronto: House of Anansi Press, 1972).
4 Arnold Toynbee, 'Foreword', in *A Study of History: The First Abridged One-Volume Edition – Illustrated* (Oxford, UK: Oxford University Press, 1972): 9. This publication combines his work from the 1930s onwards in one volume.

ous at that. As Albert Einstein said, 'nationalism is an infantile thing. It is the measles of mankind.'[5] In my experience nationalism, tribalism and organised religion often seem to block out reason in conversation.

The other diminution of the power of nation-states to control global governance comes in the shape of our everyday behaviour *vis-à-vis* our consumption patterns and media interactions. Both are observed, tracked, mediated by business and governments. Megadata is the new governance. It's not democracy and it can easily by corrupted soundlessly and unknowingly, while we sleep. The biggest part of megadata is metadata. It is not the private bits or the secret conversations about bombs, sex or politics that matter, but the metadata capture of the when, where, who of our lives that tell business and government what we're about, who we talk to, what we consume, what time we go to bed, and where we sleep. As the former CIA operative Edward Snowden said in 2014: 'Metadata does not lie . . . you can trust the metadata . . . metadata's often more intrusive [than megadata].'[6]

Megadata capture and analysis relies on algorithmic analysis which is essentially digital. Yet we remain analogic: emotional, rational and irrational, metaphoric, eulogistic, ecstatic, sexual, aesthetic, moral beings – and sometimes wrong. As Nobel prize-winning economist Daniel Kahneman said, we have two ways of thinking: the first is intuitive and immediate and the second

5 As quoted in George Sylvester Viereck, 'What Life Means to Einstein: An Interview by George Sylvester Viereck', *The Saturday Evening Post*, 26 October 1929: 117.

6 Alan Rusbridger and Ewen MacAskill, 'Edward Snowden Interview: The Edited Transcript', *The Guardian*, 18 July 2014; www.theguardian.com/world/2014/jul/18/-sp-edward-snowden-nsa-whistleblower-interview-transcript.

is thoughtful, reflective and analytical.[7] We live, we evolve, we adapt, and all by learning. We learn, and have evolved, by making mistakes, but there are no mistakes in megadata capture. As Edward Snowden has observed, you're either in or out: there's no halfway in the digitised world. So, what does the nation-state matter when our every action is monitored by national governments and by supraterritorial corporations?

In the virtual world, which an increasing number of people inhabit continually, it matters which effective rather than affective tribe we belong to, and what technology that tribe has at its disposal. The virtual world is often empatheticless and asocial. The habitués play games with themselves, shop online, and grow obese on their self-infatuation (as there are no buttresses to social correction) and consume fast food sold to them by companies that know all about their bad habits and their basic greed for salt, sugar and fat. From pre-industrial muscle to mechanisation to digitisation to the end of human possibility. It has been suggested that just as we are reaching the end of our physical longevity potential – medicine has taken us so far and can take us no further – we will morph into the computer machines we have made in our own image.

Both government and business govern and manage by monitoring, sweeping up deviants and nudging us to conform as citizens and consumers. Governance becomes more like flying an unstable aircraft by sweeping up and analysing mega- and metadata. On the plus side, mega- and metadata allow a better understanding of the fact that society is a series of nested networks with lives of their own – interrelated, interactive but complex adaptive systems.

7 Daniel Kahneman, *Thinking Fast and Slow* (London: Allen Lane, 2011).

Seeing the Earth for the first time

I'm at WOMAD in the beautiful city of Adelaide, South Australia. WOMAD stands for the World of Music And Dance and was started in 1980 by Genesis singer Peter Gabriel who lives just outside Bath in England. To say that I am confused by what is on display here today would be an understatement of postmodernism. The band now playing, Hanggai, are a Mongolian–Chinese punk-rock six-piece using a mixture of instruments that derive from around the world through thousands of years. It's loud, invasive, incessant and compelling. Of greatest interest to me are the embedded references to calls across the Mongolian steppes, to rhythms that are not of standard rock music, and the use of ancient musical instruments to thump out the defiance that is punk music. The lead singer has stripped to the waist. He's paunchy, and doesn't quite have the vocality of Elvis Presley, the gyrations of Mick Jagger or the athleticism of Chris Martin or Iggy Pop. He sings in English and Mongolian: the crowd loves the mélange; such is their thirst for things exotic and their cosmopolitanism. The band says their influences include Pink Floyd, Neil Diamond and Radiohead as well as punk and Mongolian folk songs. There is an issue of identity here, or is this the coming alternative global homogeneity, so derided when it's McDonald's 'I'm lovin' it', Microsoft's Windows, or Starbucks' 'all-coffee-tastes-the-bland-same' cultural invasion? Is pop and rock the real global homogeneity? Is this globalism (the spread of global ideas) the real globality?

One of the progenitors of punk I referred to earlier, Malcolm McLaren, said that punk heralded a new age of the conspicuous consumption of ideas, rather than the conspicuous consumption of things: a shift from having to being and doing, a rebalancing of yin and yang. With Hanggai we have the conspicuous consumption of global ideas hung around a punk-rock drumbeat with soft references to exoticism for easy Western ears.

The modern globality revolution started in the US – they took the pictures of the Earth from the Moon and gave birth to rock 'n' roll – but was carried forward and given momentum by the availability of bananas 24/7, intercontinental ballistic missiles and The Beatles. When John Lennon said in March 1966 that The Beatles were more popular than Jesus (but that both would die), their records were burned in some US states. But he was actually talking about globalism: their music was being listened to everywhere, by everyone.[8] It was casteless and classless, it was catchy and memorable, and it spoke of everyday concerns – love, the planet, and humanity.

In the twenty-first century Lennon's song 'Imagine' is as potent a revolutionary message as Karl Marx's pamphlets and books or Charles Darwin and Alfred Wallace Russell's evolutionary theory. Lennon was as reviled and loved then as evolutionary theory is disputed by some reactionary conservatives today. Similarly, the universality of human rights is often denied today.

In a sense, Václav Havel summed up the idea of globality in *Summer Meditations*, which was quoted earlier: 'the idea that the world might actually be changed by the force of truth, the

---

8 'Christianity will go. It will vanish and shrink. I needn't argue about that; I'm right and I'll be proved right. We're more popular than Jesus now; I don't know which will go first, rock 'n' roll or Christianity. Jesus was all right but his disciples were thick and ordinary. It's them twisting it that ruins it for me.' Maureen Cleave, 'The John Lennon I Knew', *The Telegraph*, 5 October 2005; www.telegraph.co.uk/culture/music/rockandjazzmusic/3646983/The-John-Lennon-I-knew.html.

power of the truthful word, the strength of a free spirit, conscience, and responsibility – with no guns, no lust for power, no political wheeling and dealing' ran counter to the conflictual view of history, including, within his own sphere, that of the former communist state of Czechoslovakia, and Marxist dialectical materialism.[9]

When Václav Havel was 52, William Anders on Apollo 8 came out from behind the Moon, on 24th December 1968, and shouted:

> Oh, my God! Look at that picture over there!
>
> Here's the Earth coming up. Wow, is that pretty![10]

In 1948, just a few years after US rockets, based on German World War II V2 rockets, had roughly mapped the Earth's surface from space, Fred Hoyle, a British astronomer and writer (and the inventor of the theory of black holes and dark matter), made the observation that when we could see the Earth from beyond then a revolution in thinking would occur. That revolution, or evolutionary adaptation, is now taking place. Here is what Hoyle said in 1948:

> Once a photograph of the Earth, taken from outside, is available, we shall, in an emotional sense, acquire an additional dimension . . . Once let the sheer isolation of the Earth become plain to every man, whatever his nationality or creed, and a new idea as powerful as any in history will be let loose.

Less than twenty years later, that additional dimension became real when we saw the first photographs of Earth taken from

---

9 Havel, *Summer Meditations*: 5.
10 www-tc.pbs.org/wgbh/amex/moon/media/sf_audio_pop_01b.
 mp3.

space. These were then supplemented with the emotional and aesthetic force of photographs taken of Earthrise over the Moon. Hoyle was quoted at the time (1970):

> Well, we now have such a photograph ... Has any new idea been let loose? It certainly has. You will have noticed how suddenly everybody has become seriously concerned to protect the natural environment ... It seems to me more than a coincidence that this awareness should have happened at exactly the moment man took his first step into space.

'Earthrise', the renowned photograph that Bill Anders took in December 1968 coming round from behind the Moon on Apollo 8, is one of the most beautifully terrifying and terrifyingly beautiful, and yet at the same time life-enhancing images, Anders's photo has become the leitmotif of globality – of seeing the shared space that is planethome inhabited by the human race and all the flora and fauna we know.

Yet this image was pre-dated by a NASA photograph of the whole Earth on the front cover of the eponymous 1968 *Whole Earth Catalog*, published by Stewart Brand. Apart from a full-colour picture of the Earth (taken in 1967 from a NASA ATS-3 weather and communications satellite in a 34.047 km orbit above Earth), the *Catalog* included tips on building your own tipi and geodesic dome, growing beans, making your first computer, masturbation, taking LSD, rearing pigs and public speaking. The front cover had a photograph of the Earth and the back cover of an open road with the words 'Stay Hungry, Stay Foolish'.

The *Catalog* was a printed, pre-computer, pre-internet guide to personal empowerment and scientific enlightenment through personal learning, and one of the first references to the personal computer. It sold 2 million copies. In 2005 Steve Jobs of Apple, in an address at Stanford University, described the *Catalog* as 'one of the bibles my generation'. Brand and Jobs subscribe to the same evolutionary theory: namely, that we are prisoners of our lengthy past as stardust left over from exploding supernovae, but that we can learn to do things differently. They would subscribe to the ancient Hindu philosophy that 'the gods are later than creation'. As Brand said in 2013, 'lots of people try and change human nature but it's a waste of time. You can't change human nature but you can change tools, you can change techniques' and that way 'you can change civilisation'.[11] Jobs is reputed to have had the back cover of the *Catalog* framed in his office.

Bill Anders famously said of his Earthrise picture – which, incidentally, is always depicted with a horizontal horizon, whereas the astronauts saw it at 90°, with the Earth rising over the right side of the Moon – 'we came all this way to explore the Moon, and the most important thing is that we discovered the Earth'.[12]

In the face of a rapacious model of industrial growth, Carl Sagan asked, poignantly, 'Who will speak for Planet Earth?' And many scientists from Einstein to Hawking would echo Rachel Carson's thought that 'those who contemplate the beauty of the earth find resources of strength that will endure as long as life lasts'. Sagan's answer to his rhetorical question was that 'our loyalties are to the species and the planet. We

---

11 Stewart Brand, quoted in Carole Cadwallader, 'Hippy, Radical, Genius, Visionary ... And the First Man in Cyberspace', *The Observer*, 5 May 2013: 8-11.

12 Ron Judd, 'With a View from beyond the Moon: An Astronaut Talks Religion, Politics and Possibilities', *Seattle Times*, 7 December 2012.

speak for Earth. Our obligation to survive is owed not just to ourselves but also to that Cosmos, ancient and vast, from which we spring'.[13]

The growth of globality

A brief history of the sense of one shared space, known here as globality, fails to do justice to the many ancient philosophers and religions that always recognised the oneness of all humanity and the cosmos and the interrelations between all living and non-living matter.

Recently (in terms of the history of humanity or the universe), the European Renaissance (C14–C17) provided a bridge between a period of deep superstition and one of observation and empiricism as a tool of learning and expanded mental consciousness. This is often referred to as the rebirth of culture through art, literature and music, and was partially enabled by the development of paper and printing industries. The Renaissance reintroduced classical (Greek and Roman) thinking as the foundations of knowledge.

During this period the Polish mathematician Nicolaus Copernicus (1473–1543) created hysteria among the elites and challenged the status quo by asserting, based on observation, that the Earth goes round the sun, and not vice versa, which in turn suggested that Man may not be the font of all knowledge and the centre of the universe (although some men still think they are!).

13 Carl Sagan, 'Who Speaks for Earth?' [video], *YouTube*, bit. ly/1b7rSLF, accessed 5 February 2014.

The Italian physicist, mathematician and Renaissance man Galileo Galilei (1564–1642) through his work with telescopes provided substantial evidence in support of the Copernican revolution. He, like Copernicus, was ostracised by the established church – the status quo – for challenging their intellectual authority. They conceded finally, very begrudgingly – and did not formally admit their error until 1992! All things are relative to each other, as the Earth is to the sun, he said. In the twenty-first century the same church shows a similar intransigence in admitting to its own institutional paedophilia.

Isaac Newton, a Briton (1642–1727), is renowned for documenting the laws of motion and universal gravitation, and furthering the development of the microscope, which naturally led to further investigation of micro perspectives; along with Leibniz, he is credited with inventing calculus. Unlike the movements of the planets, the concept of gravity wasn't seen as heretical; Newton described himself as a 'natural philosopher': a title we might reinvent in the twenty-first century as 'natural scientist', as we try to rediscover transdisciplinarity in all research and enlightened thinking to solve complex problems. Today, although his discoveries are challenged, his way of thinking that all matters worthy of consideration are mechanical is under attack, as this approach leaves out sensitivities, relativities, unknowns and perturbations. And, of course, gravity is relative to the situation: true sometimes but also, as we now know, bendable.

The period from the 1630s through to 1800 is regarded as the age of Enlightenment or the Age of Reason; the latter is also the title of a pamphlet by Thomas Paine. Paine argued against the political power of the Christian church and in favour of scepticism as a form of thinking and as a way of seeing the Christian Bible as a useful and informed narrative, rather than the literal truth. Truth was drawn from scientific analysis and reasoning. He thus promoted the idea of a balance between science and awe: one promotes and lives in harmony with the other.

Thomas Malthus (1766–1834), a British and early political economist, linked economics to social issues, specifically population, sustenance, resilience and globality. He was incorrect in his prognosis that the world would run out of food for an expanding population, as he did not take into account developments in agricultural technology and the relationship between evolution, adaptation and learning. Today his ideas are being resurrected because the core of his argument is worthwhile: that the convergence of population, climate change and neoliberalism are producing a paradox – daily malnutrition for perhaps one-third of the world and obesity for another third. A tablet to his memory in Bath Abbey refers to his seminal role in developing a sophisticated model of economics which acknowledges that all economics is complex and political.

The period from the 1820s onwards has seen the application of science and the accelerating speed of technological developments, the exploitation of the Earth's lithosphere, and new models of industrial capitalism coupled with the dramatic growth of supraterritorial corporations who know no national boundaries or loyalties. Whereas empire had meant capture and control of whole continents and nation-states, from 1945 onwards empire has tended to mean spheres of influence and capture by trade, consumerism and military oversight and overflight.

Referring to the first photographs of Earth from space in the 1960s, historian Arnold Toynbee was optimistic that this oneness, this wholeness of view, this unified view of planethome, meant that 'historical horizons have been rolled back during this century, opening the way for [Man] to achieve an "ecumenical" vision of all the civilisations [he] has created'.[14]

The seen, virtual and felt world

Today in central Sydney, here and now, the day around me is people, computer screens, cups of coffee, flowers and trees, images, ideas, and hard and soft surfaces. But there are other worlds that technology has released for us to see. I can look out at the universe and wonder but I can also see the same world by looking more closely into myself or into the frangipani flower that sits in a bowl on my desk. Either way, outward or inward, I will experience a sensory overload as my mind tries to make sense of the information that my eye sees and my brain tries to interpret.

Eugene Cernan, the last of twelve men to walk on the moon (yes, they have all been men), said that 'nothing prepares you for the sensory overload you get from spacewalking'. There is a problem, he says, with the 'inability of astronauts to really communicate what we see in space'.[15]

Gaspard-Félix Tournachon, also known as Nadar, was the first to take photographs from above the Earth – in his case from a balloon over Paris – on 26th May 1863. He, like Anders and Newton, opened new worlds to explore both physical and mental landscapes. And it is what is not photographed as well as what is photographed that is interesting. Julian Barnes, 2011 Booker prize-winner, in *Levels of Life* wrote of Nadar that 'his

14 Toynbee, *A Study of History*: 29.
15 Eugene Cernan, 'This Much I Know', *Observer Magazine*, 16 June 2002: 6.

photos were as disturbing as they were beautiful: and they remain so today. To look at ourselves from afar, to make the subjective suddenly objective: this gives us psychic shock.'[16]

Exactly 150 years later Chris Hadfield posted to Twitter photographs he had taken during his six months in a Soyuz space station circling the planet. Hadfield wrote of the 'agonizingly beautiful Australian Outback' and of the sight of an erupting Mount Etna: 'Our Earth is mostly liquid rock. We live on a thin crust, with occasional hot spots.'

Hadfield's photographs are not shocking in the sense that they were the first pictures from space, but they are enlightening because they give us fresh perspectives. Particularly, as with all space photographs, territorial boundaries are non-existent, new patterns emerge of the beauty of the Earth, and human impact can be seen in all its spread. Look, for instance, at the world's largest urban agglomeration, Tokyo, with 37 million people, or the numerous condensation trails across the USA from jet traffic – enough to change the weather below. This became even more apparent immediately after 9/11/01 when all USA air traffic was curtailed following the attacks on New York's Twin Towers and the skies cleared for a day; the heavens could be seen more clearly – and space satellites could see the USA more clearly.

What we see and don't see, and is not discussed, are also pertinent in this discussion on the growing global sense of globality. It has been commented on that, despite the fact that in the late sixteenth and early seventeenth centuries Europe was wracked by plague, Shakespeare's plays only mention this health affliction twice. This is because it was so commonplace;

---

16 Emma Brockes, 'Julian Barnes: The Sense of Another Ending', *The Guardian*, 30 March 2013; www.theguardian.com/books/2013/mar/30/julian-barnes-sense-of-another-ending.

during his lifetime plague halved the population of Europe. It was also common for children to die before they reached five years old, and for many women to die in childbirth. It is for this reason – the idea of impermanency – that, at the birth of photography, photographers like Nadar tended not to take pictures of children because they were likely to die. Most of his pictures, and of other photographers at that time, are of adults who were more likely to survive.[17]

How is the world, and, just as important, how do we see it, what do we know, what do we know we don't know, and how confident are we about knowing that we know that there are things we can't even think of?

We are hell-bent on action, rather than meditation and reflection, and knowing how we know is not one of the West's strengths, partly because of our masculine, pioneering, frontier-chasing approach to life. And, as Humberto Maturana and Francisco Varela, the authors of *The Tree of Knowledge*, say, 'underlying everything we say is this constant awareness that the phenomenon of knowing cannot be taken as though there were "facts" or objects out there that we can grasp and store in our head'.[18] Others have made this same point, but from a different position. Physicist Rupert Sheldrake, who, over the last forty years, has pioneered research on morphic resonance (the fields that link everything, particularly living beings), says that 'the orthodoxy of materialism which has dominated science is crumbling ... we are beginning to understand the

17 Graham Robb, The Discovery of France: A Historical Geography (London: W.W. Norton, 2007); referenced by Will Self, 'Picture This', *New Statesman*, 22–28 March 2013: 51.

18 Humberto R. Maturana and Francisco Varela, *The Tree of Knowledge: The Biological Roots of Human Understanding* (London and Boston: Shambala, rev. edn, 1998): 25.

world beyond objectification . . . it is a world of networks and fields';[19] it is a world of expanded consciousness.

We increasingly live in a globally networked world, which may lead to expanded consciousness. Networks are the oldest organising form and have always been at the heart of humanity's main strength – working together in cohesive, cooperative, sharing wholes, as societies. In recent times, atomisation has been promoted along with the idea of the 'economically rational decision-maker', but our default mode, often for survival but certainly for progress, has been in cooperative, empathetic groups. But networks are no longer just families, streets, villages, workplaces or friends but collaborations, alliances, trade links, social media 'friends', like-minded action networks and undeliberate associations that we have little or no control over and which are driven by social media, consumerism, banking or shared interest. As Steve Waddell in *Global Action Networks*[20] has shown, many of these new networks are adaptive systems that have loose edges, myriad connections, variable outcomes, and interconnectednesses that we can hardly imagine. Their purview is unknown.

Our networked world, one of the characteristics of which has been that information is free (along with the perception that much else is also free!), is also increasingly being co-opted by business models that make use of this 'free' information about every individual's behaviour, purchasing habits, sexual preferences, dietary quirks and personal relationships. We are increasingly being fed back mirror images of ourselves which reassure us, encourage us to sink further into consumerism, and

19 Rupert Sheldrake, 'Earth Talk: Science and Spiritual Practices' [video], *YouTube*, 2014; bit.ly/1yORnui, accessed 13 March 2014.
20 Steve Waddell, *Global Action Networks: Creating Our Future Together* (London: Palgrave Macmillan, 2011).

make us more dependent, and less alone. Marshall McLuhan's 'global village' has arrived, and, just like in the local village, everyone knows your game, and your name. Everyone's a 'friend' on Facebook even if real empathy may be on short supply in a too-busy world.[21] The difference between the real village and the global village is that now we have many *effective* communities but no so many *affective* communities. We know more people but are further apart.

Jaron Lanier, who among many things coined the term 'personal computer', says that information can only be free while there are other ways of making money but as soon as it becomes the dominant wealth creation device, or form of capital, it will be charged for. As he says: 'your lack of privacy is someone else's wealth'.[22] Furthermore, he makes the point that the search engine company Google are digitising the world's printed literature not for some altruistic goal but because the ultimate objective is artificial intelligence. (This is already happening: however much I try to reprogramme this MacBook Pro to let me write in English, it continues to ask me to correct back to Amglish or some strange limited Globlish.)

They will feed back the distilled knowledge containing all that the software has learnt and call it wisdom, at which point thinking will die because we will apparently have thought everything there is to think. Already a whole generation of Gen X and Y are addicted to social media and cannot operate without signing in regularly. This is the ultimate control by a private

21 Roman Krznaric, 'Is Australia losing its empathy?', *The Guardian*, 25 February 2014; www.theguardian.com/culture/australia-culture-blog/2014/feb/26/is-australia-losing-its-empathy, accessed 28 November 2014.

22 Jaron Lanier, *Who Owns The Future?* (London: Allen Lane, 2013): 3.

company. Recently, many of the largest international social media companies, most notably US-invented Facebook, Twitter, Google and Microsoft, have been found wanting in their payment of national taxes. But they are not alone and the same can be said of Richard Branson's Virgin empire, Rupert Murdoch's News Corp, and Starbucks. The empire strikes back at you for buying in to them and their products.

The role of the international corporation is central to understanding the twenty-first century. They, as much as nation-states, can make or break us.

The nation-state is challenged for legitimacy by transnational corporations, or, as I have previously termed them, 'supra-territorial corporations' or STCs. The nation-state now records populations, transactions (if it can), collects taxes (if it can), and tries to deliberate on how the world should or might be in multilateral forums such as the various branches of the United Nations. Theories of power now wrestle with the accountability and governance of corporate entitles whose legitimacy rests in their ability to play national regimes, commoditise and marketise whatever will sell, and circumvent rules written for a world of international trade rather than corporate empires. This is not as new a situation as many would believe; in the 1870s the British government had to ask permission of the British East India company (which it had established by Act of Parliament) if it could sail through 'their' waters and establish a penal colony in Australia.[23] Much of the British and other European colonial empires were first set up as trading zones and sources of raw materials. So, the first colonial proselytising was in trade and wealth creation, which was swiftly followed by the Christian church and the values of Western 'civilisation'.

23 Michael Pembroke, *Arthur Phillip: Sailor, Mercenary, Governor, Spy* (Melbourne and London: Hardie Grant Books, 2013).

Despite the decolonisation of much of the world over the last one hundred years, the world as it is so constructed today is very much the result of European colonisation and the promotion of a model of pioneer, resource-demand, profit-driven model economics and capitalism. And this is the model that the new worlds of first the Asian Tigers led by Japan, and now Brazil, Russia, Turkey, Indonesia and China have adopted. We are all consumers of brands, planned obsolescence and apparently free knowledge.[24] As Lanier notes, the Catholic Church has been into social engineering for more than 2,000 years and now it is the turn of Facebook and Google, whose naïve motto is 'Don't be evil'. So their mission is much the same: to connect, to sell to, to adopt as users and to promote goodness(!)[25] Not necessarily.

Transitions

In my transition from a miserablist to an optimist there have been many moments of clarity. One of the most profound is the idea that, if the idea of sustainability (and permanence) is a product of the affluent society, then it follows that it is not necessarily a rational question as to why humans should survive but rather a non-rational, perhaps emotional and/or moral issue. We are a unique hypothesis and this is a fantastic experiment with life on Earth. But there is no reason why we should survive, and our attempts to do so may be in vain as the forces beyond our control are just that.

24 Michael Hardt and Antonio Negri, *Empire* (Cambridge, MA: Harvard University Press, 2000).
25 Lanier, *Who Owns the Future?*: 182.

There are various formulations for understanding the epochs in the history of humankind on Earth. For some commentators we are now in the fourth age. Although these are not thought of as necessarily synchronous, the fourth age of sustainability is preceded by: agriculture, when we developed animal husbandry and crop development; industrialisation, when we developed the use of the minerals and fossils embedded in the lithosphere; and the information age, when technologies allowed information and knowledge to become the dominant drivers of change and innovation. Now we are entering the age of globality or planetary age – if we survive.

Two questions that are linked: how is the world organised in the twenty-first century, and how do we see the world? Martin Luther King said, on Christmas Eve 1967: 'If we are to have peace on earth . . . we must develop a world perspective.'[26] In 1939 Toynbee wrote, 'The challenge of being called upon to create a political world-order, the framework for an economic world-order . . . now confronts our Modern Western society.'[27] I am convinced that from a macro perspective human history is as one: we have one history as a biological and moral species on planet Earth.

David Cannadine in his 2013 book *The Undivided Past* points out that we divide ourselves against each other, particularly in the case of politics where those who crave power seek

---

26 Martin Luther King, 'Beyond Vietnam', speech, Riverside Church, New York City, 4 April 1967; mlk-kpp01.stanford.edu/index.php/encyclopedia/encyclopedia/enc_beyond_vietnam_4_april_1967, accessed 28 November 2014.
27 Toynbee, 'Foreword', in *A Study of History*: 10.

to create conflict rather than harmony: harmony does not get you elected and does not serve the sociopathic tendencies of those who tend to want power. He quotes Maya Angelou:

> I note the obvious differences
> Between each sort and type,
> But we are more alike, my friends,
> Than we are unalike.[28]

Our historic narratives tend to divide in order to categorise based on religion, nation, class, gender, race and civilisation – the last category being the most problematic. On the cusp of radical evolution and adaptation-or-perish, the idea that the current model of rapacious pioneering industrialisation is 'civilised' begs many questions. Wouldn't a more 'civilised' society be one where resources were, as a matter of principle, conserved and where the model of private acquisition automatically included a principle of an absolute maximum gain and some absolute minimum amount of redistribution?

Toynbee said that civilisations were born out of challenges of all sorts and that it is 'creative minorities' that create new ideas within society. He again stressed, from a macro perspective, the commonality in our shared history. This idea, combined with our growing sense of globality, truly makes this the age of Pax Interdependence or the planetary age.

This book is concerned with *human* evolution, adaptation and learning, but it is worth noting that much contemporary discussion is about whether humans can withstand what some are thinking of as the coming *natural* extinction. This apocalyptic scenario is predicated on the previous five great extinctions over millions of years. The first, the Ordovician–Silurian mass extinction destroyed almost all life in the oceans, as that

28 Cannadine, *The Undivided Past*: 6

was where most life existed at the time (between about 450 and 440 million years ago). The second, the Late Devonian mass extinction, took several million years to take effect and again destroyed most sea life, including the reefs. The third, the Permian mass extinction (about 252 million years ago) destroyed some 96% of all marine life on Earth, 70% of terrestrial vertebrate species, and some 57% of all insect families and 83% of all insect genera; the remainder providing the foundation for all the life that now exists here. The fourth, the Triassic–Jurassic mass extinction (201 million years ago) seems to have been caused either by an asteroid, climate change or volcanic eruptions. The Cretacious–Paleogene mass extinction, the fifth (66 million years ago), is the one that many people are most familiar with because it wiped out the dinosaurs along with some three-quarters of all plant and animal species.

If we are not first wiped out by a lone madman with a nuclear bomb, we may be on the verge of the next mass extinction – the sixth, the Anthropocene extinction, caused by a combination of events which includes the release of carbon into the atmosphere by humans making the Earth an even more hostile environment to inhabit. We already live in a thin margin between arid desert, ice plateau and deep sea and we may have made life in this thin sliver even less feasible. The science says that this century, and perhaps the next few decades, will tell.

But back to the short period of human history. I have previously cited a number of historians and geographers including David Cannadine, Jared Diamond and Arnold Toynbee as interesting and hopefully useful examples of ways of seeing human history. Here, now, are a few more contemporaneous modellers of human evolution, adaptation and learning.

Richard Cassells, a former museum director, in his design for a Sustainability Museum, lists thirteen ages of humankind starting 2.5 million years ago and ending with a post-industri-alisation age, beyond the current age of sustainability.[29] There is more than a touch of the Utopian in his categorisations and he doesn't go forward to a post-Earth section, but then he's a former museum director, not a futurist, even if he's an optimist.

MOSET: the Museum of Social and Environmental Transformations
Richard Cassells (2012)

The chronological galleries
The galleries are dedicated to 12 global systemic transformations which are considered most relevant to Western history in general.
- The Tool-making Revolution (from 2.5 MYBP)
- The Second Human Revolution (from 100,000 BP)
- The First Agricultural Revolution (from 10,000 BCE)
- The First Urban Revolution (from 4500 BCE)
- The First Imperial Revolution (from 2500 BCE)
- The Re-invasion of the Americas (from 1450)
- The Scientific Revolution (from 1600)
- The First Industrial Revolution (from 1750)
- The Age of Oil (from 1920)
- The Nuclear Age (from 1950)
- The Digital Revolution (from 1980)
- The Sustainability Revolution (from 2005)

29 Richard Cassells, 'The Devil is in the Synergy. The Exhibitions at MOSET: A Hypothetical Museum of Human Transitions', in Malcolm McIntosh (ed.), *The Necessary Transition: The Journey towards the Sustainable Enterprise Economy* (Sheffield, UK: Greenleaf Publishing, 2013): 51-79.

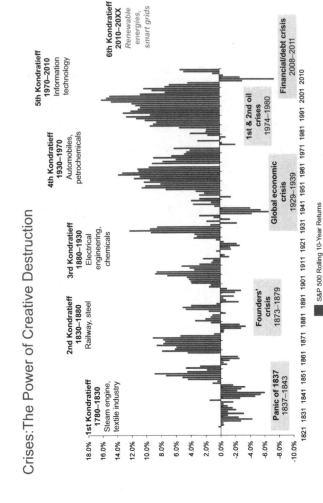

Crises:The Power of Creative Destruction

Source: Allianz Global Investors, Germany's Global Fund Manager, *The 6th Kondratieff: Long Waves of Prosperity: Capital Market Analysis.*
Based on stock market data used in Robert J. Shiller, *Irrational Exuberance* (Princeton, NJ: Princeton University Press, 2005); Datastream; Allianz
Global Investors Capital Market and Thematic Research, December 2013. Reproduced by kind permission of Allianz Global Investors.

I have said that my observations, working globally, are that change comes through ideas, technologies and institutions. Carlota Perez is interested in the relationship between technology and finance. She says there have been five industrial revolutions, based on these two variables, but her observations are based within the period of the industrial revolution: in other words, the last 250 years.

The industries and infrastructures of each technological revolution

First

- From 1771: the 'industrial revolution'; Britain
- Mechanised cotton industry
- Wrought iron
- Machinery
- Canals and waterways
- Turnpike roads
- Water power (highly improved water wheels)

Second

- From 1829
- Age of steam and railways
- In Britain and spreading to Continental Europe and USA
- Steam engines and machinery (made from iron; fuelled by coal)
- Iron and coal mining (now playing a central role in growth)
- Railway construction
- Rolling stock production
- Steam power for many industries (including textiles)
- Railways (use of steam engine)

- Universal postal service
- Telegraph (mainly nationally along railway lines)
- Great ports, great depots and worldwide sailing ships
- City gas

Third

- From 1875
- Age of steel, electricity and heavy engineering
- USA and Germany overtaking Britain
- Cheap steel (especially Bessemer)
- Full development of steam engine for steel ships
- Heavy chemistry and civil engineering
- Electrical equipment industry
- Copper and cables
- Canned and bottled food
- Paper and packaging
- Worldwide shipping in rapid steel steamships (use of Suez Canal)
- Worldwide railways (use of cheap steel rails and bolts in standard sizes)
- Great bridges and tunnels
- Worldwide telegraph
- Telephone (mainly nationally)
- Electrical networks (for illumination and industrial use)

Fourth

- From 1908
- Age of oil, the automobile and mass production
- In USA and spreading to Europe
- Mass-produced automobiles
- Cheap oil and oil fuels
- Petrochemicals (synthetics)

- Internal combustion engine for automobiles, transport, tractors, aeroplanes, war tanks and electricity
- Home electrical appliances
- Refrigerated and frozen foods
- Networks of roads, highways, ports and airports
- Networks of oil ducts
- Universal electricity (industry and homes)
- Worldwide analogue telecommunications (telephone, telex and cablegram): wire and wireless

Fifth

- From 1971
- Age of information and telecommunications
- In USA, spreading to Europe and Asia
- The information revolution:
  - Cheap microelectronics
  - Computers, software
  - Telecommunications
  - Control instruments
  - Computer-aided biotechnology and new materials
  - World digital telecommunications (cable, fibre-optics, radio and satellite)
  - Internet/electronic mail and other e-services
- Multiple source, flexible-use, electricity networks
- High-speed physical transport links (by land, air and water)

Sixth

- From 2003
- Age of cleantech and biotech
- In USA and Europe going global
- Renewable energy led by solar, wind and biofuels
- Energy efficiency

- Energy storage technologies
- Electric vehicles
- Nanomaterials
- Synthetic biology
- Enhanced electricity transmission capabilities
- Decentralisation of power generation
- Connection of electricity and transportation energy infrastructures
- Demand-response management
- Increased availability of water and electricity
- Extensive gene databanks

Sources: Carlota Perez, *Technological Revolutions and Financial Capital: The Dynamics of Bubbles and Golden Ages* (London: Edward Elgar Publishing, 2003); Merrill Lynch, *The Sixth Revolution: The Coming of Cleantech*; www.responsible-investor.com/images/uploads/resources/research/21228316156Merril_Lynch-_the_coming_of_clean_tech.pdf

Not only is the revolution this time being televised and zapped around the world instantaneously by various social media – so that everyone has their 15 minutes (or seconds) of fame. This revolution, or rapid evolution, requires a dramatic shift in the modes of behaviour and thinking attached to the last 250 years of industrial, fossil-fuel-led capitalism.

This time we need more energy, but from renewable sources. And energy production is becoming more decentralised in its generation, and distributed more through microgrids and distributed storage facilities. The best evidence is that renewables are competitive pricewise if whole costs are included – which includes the cost of carbon pricing and climate change risk amelioration. But, until those costs are included and until we can overcome the fact that fossil fuels (and in particular coal) are the best storage of energy that currently exists, fossil fuels will continue to dominate the energy generation market.

The current challenge of change is significant and Thomas Malthus is relevant, albeit a little premature in his prediction. Population resource use has outpaced sensible resource use. We really are at a point where Marx was spot on in saying that 'Men make their own history, but they do not make it as they please . . . but under circumstances existing already, given and transmitted from the past.'[30] The 'circumstances existing already' rely largely on hydrocarbon deposits laid down over the last 3.5 billion years and rapidly released over the last 250 years. The release of these carbon deposits is necessary to distribute energy, pollution and financial wealth unequally globally. Now we need a more resilient, low-carbon-intensive energy and wealth distribution system that is equitable and low-cost to all. Clean water, basic healthcare, housing and education should become essential human rights along with freedom of speech and the rule of law.

In *Just Transitions* Mark Swilling and Eve Anneke caution that apparently progressive transitions can lead to the opposite of the desired or anticipated results.[31] The role of adaptive leadership in reaching consensus between divided camps of thought is highlighted in their reference to the work of John Grin and colleagues who emphasise the need to understand a 'Multi-Level Perspective' in thinking about systems change focusing on the 'co-evolution of technological change', 'multi-actor

30 Karl Marx, *The Eighteenth Brumaire of Louis Bonaparte*, 1852; https://www.marxists.org/archive/marx/works/1852/18th-brumaire/ch01.htm, accessed 16 December 2014.

31 Mark Swilling and Eve Annecke, *Just Transitions: Explorations of Sustainability in an Unfair World* (United Nations University Press, 2012).

processes' and 'reconfiguring institutional and organisational structures'.[32]

Safa Motesharrei and colleagues at the US National Science Foundation have developed a cross-disciplinary model known as 'Human And Nature DYnamical' (HANDY)[33] – which taking a macro perspective shows that even advanced, complex civilisations are susceptible to collapse, which begs questions about the sustainability of modern civilisation. The crucial factors seem to be population, climate, water, agriculture and energy. The possible convergence of two of these factors could lead to collapse: 'the stretching of resources due to the strain placed on the ecological carrying capacity'; and 'the economic stratification of society into Elites [rich] and Masses (or "Commoners") [poor]'. This sounds remarkably like the situation Graeber and Piketty have written about with the 1/99% division of wealth and the rise in inequality caused by the new machine and digital age which strips whole layers of middle agents or workers out of employment possibilities.[34]

In *Sapiens: A Brief History of Humankind* Israeli historian Yuval Harari largely ignores the ongoing tribal conflict on his doorstep while arguing that Sapiens beat back and defeated all other human variants over the last 150,000 years and Sapiens

---

32 John Grin, Jan Rotmans and Johan Schot, *Transitions to Sustainable Development: New Directions in the Study of Long Term Transformative Change* (New York and London: Routledge, 2010).

33 Safa Motesharrei, Jorge Rivas and Eugenia Kalnay, 'Human and Nature Dynamics (HANDY): Modeling Inequality and Use of Resources in the Collapse or Sustainability of Societies', *Ecological Economics* 101 (May 2014): 90-102.

34 Erik Brynjolfsson and Andrew McAfee, *The Second Machine Age: Work, Progress, and Prosperity in a Time of Brilliant Technologies* (New York and London: Norton, 2014).

– us – are naturally aggressive, conflictual and tribal.[35] But, along with Steven Pinker (referred to later), he agrees we have learnt how to be a significantly more peaceful species than we have ever been before, despite the fact that we have a tendency for elites and masses. Part of our evolution has been to correct these two tendencies – to war, and to wealth and power division. Evolution, learning – and then adaptation.

The HANDY report highlights a situation which today is being seen as the 1/99% distribution of wealth. The authors' long-term historical analysis seems pertinent to today: '. . . accumulated surplus is not evenly distributed throughout society, but rather has been controlled by an elite. The mass of the population, while producing the wealth, is only allocated a small portion of it by elites, usually at or just above subsistence levels.'[36]

He Ping (和平) are the Chinese characters for peace. 和 is a combination of two characters that stand for grain and mouths. 平 means even, level or balanced. 和平 is therefore the even distribution of grain or sustenance among the people, or justice.

35 Yuval Harari, *Sapiens: A Brief History of Humankind* (London: Harvil Sekker, 2014).
36 Nafeez Ahmeed, 'Nasa-Funded Study: Industrial Civilisation Headed for "Irreversible Collapse"?', *The Guardian*, 14 March 2014; www.theguardian.com/environment/earth-insight/2014/ mar/14/nasa-civilisation-irreversible-collapse-study-scientists.

Occupy and global governance

It is unseasonably warm for November in London and I am sitting out at Gabriel's Wharf on the Thames Embankment drinking Italian beer served by a young man who says he's a Kurd from Turkey. He is escaping the draft by sending home cash every year to help the Turkish government so that he doesn't help oppress his own people by being in the military. The European Union means he can work anywhere in the world's largest economy with its flexible labour laws, even though Turkey is not yet a member. He has a Master's degree in media studies but can earn more as a waiter in London than in his chosen profession in Istanbul. The fifteen or so staff at the gourmet pizza restaurant represent fifteen nationalities; they are the cosmopolitan melting pot that is London and many other world cities.[37]

Over the river is the headquarters of Unilever running its tentacles out to 156 markets. Beyond their corporate headquarters is St Paul's Cathedral, figurative headquarters to the global Anglican community and on this day home to OLSX (Occupy London Stock Exchange). Both are places of moral confusion. Unilever's current leader is Paul Polman (he may not be by the

---

37 I have lived in Brisbane, Queensland, Australia, a city that has a doubled its population in the last 35 years which now stands at 2 million, 50% of whom were not born in Australia. For Australia as a whole, 42% of the population were not born in Australia and 30% are non-white. The transformation since the end of the apartheid White Australia policy in the 1970s is enormous, even if there is still a xenophobic fear of an Asian invasion from the top end and significant racial discrimination against the Aboriginal and Torres Strait Island peoples who arrived 50,000 years before the European invasion.

time you read this book, so rapid is the change in leadership in many large companies, but his work and the work of Unilever in the early twenty-first century will remain exemplary for many years to come), who has embarked on the visionary mission of doubling the company's business without increasing its use of the Earth's resources. By 2014 nearly 100,000 people in more than 150 markets around the world had signed up to monitor and report on their progress in his company's direction.

On the way I've wandered into Foyles, the bookshop, and wondered about buying the new biography of Steve Jobs, but decide just at the last moment that of course I should be downloading the ebook! I search the index and find no references to social democracy, corporate responsibility or sustainability. For him, with all his insights and Zen Buddhism, social democracy, corporate responsibility and sustainability were reputational issues and not the concerns of global business – as far as I can see from the book – and this despite Jobs and Bill Gates having been born out of the swamp of Californian seventies hippiedom. Perhaps this is more evidence that love, peace and happiness were just selfish rather than collective aspirations in some cultures.

St Paul's is now floodlit across the river. No Damascene conversion for St Steve here. The twenty-first century poses a metacognition challenge. How do we organise knowledge and our minds? Indeed, sorting out the situation we have created on Earth can only be done if we re-see the world in the light of rethinking our minds and how we see our minds from an evolutionary perspective. Martin Rees, the cosmologist, makes the point that if there was intelligent life in space humans might not be able to recognise it because we have not evolved to a high enough level to recognise other intelligences. This thought is not unlike Mahatma Gandhi's answer to the question 'what do you think of Western civilisation?' which was 'it would be a good idea!'

This chapter is concerned with re-seeing the world, because, as Donella Meadows said when discussing thinking about systems, 'we know a tremendous amount about how the world works, but not nearly enough. Our knowledge is amazing, our ignorance even more so.'[38] In wandering around the world and interviewing people at Occupy sites in New York and London, and in roundtables of experts in the first decades of the twenty-first century, what struck me most was not a sense of certainty about how the world is, but how much people did not know about how the world would be, could be or how it got to where it is now. The not-knowingness was palpable. In a sense, the cry from the streets is one of seeing the world for the first time and not recognising it: an anguished cry from the heart in the face of endless time and space, a scream into the universe at the perpetual mystery of life, and most of all 'My goodness, now that we know a little, how did we get to this place and what shall we do?' 'I am free but I am powerless.'

In the 1980s and '90s I worked for BBC Television as a journalist on current affairs, natural history and features, and my instinct for solid empirical evidence to support theories remains stronger than ever – a point I am always impressing on PhD candidates and which is a primary concern in reading 'scholarly' academic articles. But often I am surprised by the lack of up-to-date or reliable evidence cited by the ivory-towered. Most often common sense is defied, but the desire satisfied, particularly in the social sciences, to develop a new theory at the expense of the evidence.

38 Donella H. Meadows, *Thinking in Systems: A Primer* (White River Junction, VT: Chelsea Green Publishing, 2008): ch. 4.

I am in accord with the BBC's veteran Middle East reporter Jeremy Bowen, who in 2014 said that 'visits to presidential palaces, foreign ministries and embassies all matter, but being on the streets is the best way to get to the heart of the matter'.[39] It was Philip Graham of the *Washington Post* who popularised the phrase that 'journalism is the first rough draft of history'. In 2010 and 2011, with this in mind, I took time to engage in conversation for many hours with people involved in the Occupy movement in New York and London, and to a lesser extent in Boston, Paris, Bath and Tokyo. Among the insights I gained, which are discussed further in subsequent pages, were the central questions: 'How did such and such happen? How do decisions like that get made? Where is the locus of power? How were the banks bailed out? Why am I unemployed?' – which led me to put all these thoughts into one question that seemed to be at the heart of their enquiry and angst: 'How does the (social) world work or what does global governance look like?'

Similarly, in a series of roundtables I convened, held in six countries on four continents with experts in sustainable enterprise in 2009 and 2010, one issue arose around every table. This was the considerable scientific illiteracy that exists in every country about how the natural world works – about Earth systems science, particularly when it comes to climate change science. This, coupled with illiteracy concerning global governance, is very troubling at this point in history when we are reaching for global solutions to global problems.

Trust capital is very low this century. People don't trust the church, unless they live in the god-fearing societies such as the USA and the Middle East; they don't trust or believe business

39 Jeremy Bowen, 'Notebook', *New Statesman*, 7–13 March 2014: 22.

but they buy into their advertisements for the good life; they have hundreds of friends on Facebook, but on average a smaller number of close contacts than previously. Apparently, the average person has the same number of close connections as ever: about four. And the suggested cognitive limit to the number of people with whom one can maintain stable social relationships is 150[40] – a similar number to the average population of villages around the world for millennia.

Democratic capitalism is in crisis because its proponents now think that it has won as the preferred system and claim that the world is flat. The world isn't flat and indeed is very bumpy, and the number of ongoing street demonstrations around the world is testimony to this fact. The Occupy movement, the Middle East uprisings and the various almost daily demonstrations in different regions of China have common cause and are rooted in all cases in a perceived sense of injustice.

The evidence is that these grievances have three common origins. First, in an interconnected world, one community perceives another to enjoy higher wealth and better life satisfaction. This is often true but it may also be illusory. It is the downside of our neural and sometimes neurotic interconnectivity. This connectivity allows the collecting of individuals in public spaces to demonstrate their collective strength and get media attention. Second, in all cases people feel a lack of empowerment. In a global world local control and enclosure has given way to a sense that decisions are made in mysterious ways. Megadata algorithmic solutions do not lead to empowerment. Third, there is a growing awareness that the world is interconnected and that we do share one planetary space, however hard national governments may try to hang on to their

40 Known as Dunbar's number after British anthropologist Robin Dunbar.

territorial authority. How that world works, both physically and socially, is an area of mystery to most people.

Let me present some evidence from my research over the last few years. In 2009 and 2010 I ran a series of discussions in London, New York, Beijing, Sydney, Toronto and Cape Town on issues concerning the putative and in some cases emerging sustainable enterprise economy. Each roundtable of about 10–20 people was highly interactive and involved representatives from the largest of organisations in business, government and civil society and the smallest of entrepreneurs and NGOs, as well as a good transdisciplinary mix of experts from academia and other parts of society. The first six meetings heard evidence and held discussions in the House of Lords in London under the chairpersonship of Lord Michael Hastings, then with KPMG. The subsequent roundtables were held on a similar basis around the world supported variously by KPMG, Westpac Bank, the UN Global Compact and a number of universities. Since then, a number of transdisciplinary and trisector international conferences have taken place at the Eden Project and at Wessex Water in the UK, at the UN University in Tokyo and at Griffith University in Australia in support of the same aims: transdisciplinary conversations involving all sectors of society in search of common themes that transcend boundaries.

Events come and go. Some commentators have argued that the activities around the world in the 1960s achieved little, and the Occupy movement in the 2000s fizzled out without much perceivable success. But, as with the Middle East demonstrations, in each case the ability to meet and break free of the shackles of governments or corporations is a liberation; and the questions that are raised by these free and sometimes random voices echo on through social discourse long after the demonstrators have been beaten back by tear gas, truncheon, injunction, dissipation or exhaustion. It is often to these people that we owe human progress in the face of intransigence or inertia on the part of the institutions that have arisen around money, power, religion or other vested interest. Of course, sometimes such public demonstrations take us backwards or inhibit progress, as in the case of government-inspired events or rioting for new jeans or electronic equipment, both of which are witnessed as frequently nowadays as genuinely political street action.

The roundtables on sustainable enterprise held in 2009 and 2010 were not street action and were held in august institutional settings. They were attempts to measure concerns and facilitate cross-border discussions in the hope of seeing the future. Interestingly, their outcomes and the questions they raised were not dissimilar to the issues raised a few years later by the Occupy participants.

Across the world, the participants decided that the issues in need of close attention were:

- Food security: land use, soil and water, marine life

- Energy: production and use

- Resource depletion

- Transport, mobility, access

- Debt as money: debt = consumption

- Urbanisation, housing and buildings

- Population, demographics, footprints

- Climate change science

- Telecommunications, social media and knowledge

The four concerns that were common to all eleven round-tables in four continents under very different political economies are the themes that will dominate this century and should be the tableau for education, politics and governance:

- Scientific illiteracy

- Market failure

- Institutional inertia

- The leadership deficit

Most significantly, all the roundtables at some point in their lengthy discussions asked two questions, which could be seen as the subtitles for this book:

- What does it mean to be human now that we know what we know about ourselves?

- What is our relationship with the planet now that we know about the state of the planet?[41]

Wandering amongst the participants at the Occupy sites in New York and London in 2009 I realised that the central theme was identity. The media wanted to know the easy flag-waving issues; they wanted to catch a nugget and shine a light on it. 'How can we explain to people sitting comfortably on sofas at home why others are willing to sleep under canvas in the cold, harassed by the police, for what?' TV news in particular

41 For more background on the Roundtables for Sustainable Enterprise, please see Malcolm McIntosh and Sandra Waddock, 'Learning from the Roundtables on the Sustainable Enterprise Economy: The United Nations Global Compact and the Next Ten Years', in Andreas Rasche and Georg Kell (eds.), *The United Nations Global Compact: Achievements, Trends and Opportunities* (Cambridge, UK: Cambridge University Press, 2012): 215-33.

never got even close to understanding, and, writing this now, I'm watching the news and trying to get the distillation on offer as to why people in Kiev, Bangkok and Brisbane have – these are today's examples – as the bright, shiny news person is telling me, 'taken to the streets'.

I also visited Occupy camps in Bath and Paris and talked to people who had occupied other sites – there were at the height of the Occupy movement some 950 around the world – in Latin America, Japan and Germany. In all cases, the turning-out onto the streets had been by people of all ages and from all backgrounds; and all of them had one existential question about the modern world (or should I correctly label it the postmodern world?) and that was: 'How does it work?' Beyond the infrequent grand theorising, which I'll return to later, was incomprehension about how the decisions to bail out the banks, and in some cases distribute largesse to each citizen (Australia gave each adult $600 to spend), had been made. On what theoretical basis were these decisions made, who made them, and, most fundamentally, where did the money come from?

One of the fundamental issues at the heart of the age of globality is understanding both natural and social systems, and, so far, to date, most people in most places do not seem to know how it all works. John Ruggie talks about how the world 'hangs together'[42] and others talk about 'the ties that bind'. John Donne reminded us that 'no man is an island entire unto himself'[43] and in this century this is so true, but we are pulled between loving localism for its warmth and coherence while operating virtually in our daily doings. Jared Diamond's book *The World until Yesterday* talks about how we are rapidly los-

---

42 John Ruggie (ed.), *Embedding Global Markets: An Enduring Challenge* (Farnham, UK: Ashgate, 2008).

43 John Donne, 'No Man Is An Island' (1624).

ing the lessons of traditional ways of being in communities and societies that have existed for centuries and sometimes longer. In all his examples the peoples he writes about have commonality with other peoples and similar aspects of coherence, daily repetition and continual reinforcement.[44]

This is a lengthy quote from Harvard professor John Ruggie in 2012. Ruggie was the progenitor of the United Nations Global Compact with business, as well as the Millennium Development Goals when he served as Assistant Secretary-General to Kofi Annan, and latterly the principles on business and human rights.

> One critical gap lies in the realm of global governance itself: the growing misalignment between the scope and impact of globalizing forces and actors, and the capacity of societies to manage their adverse consequences. We live in tightly-coupled natural systems like the climate; we have constructed tightly-coupled economic systems like global financial markets and complex supply chains; and the number and diversity of 'problems without passports' has increased significantly. But we remain stuck attempting to manage such globally integrated systems through largely self-interested politics among and within 193 nation states, with only a thin overlay of international institutions and law . . . But what if we were to fall short? Look around and you will already see signs of some of the consequences: they take the form of resource nationalism, increased protectionism, sectarian violence, populism on the left and the right, xenophobia, homophobia – and generally

44 Jared Diamond, *The World until Yesterday: What Can We Learn from Traditional Societies?* (London: Allen Lane, 2012).

rolling back globalization out of fear of 'the other' and driven by anger for being left behind. That of course would not augur well for people, planet, or profits.[45]

Perhaps Marshall McLuhan's 'global village' is being replicated with the coherence created by every street having a McDonald's and every city having an Occupy or some similar site.[46] Perhaps, also, the baby-boomer generation have forgotten – or never knew – how the post-WWII social agreement came about, how after the great depression and two world wars liberalism was embedded in a Keynesian social contract to deliver both free global markets and some level of welfare support. Bretton Woods, the place and the metaphor, are forgotten: but, as many have commented, this social contract was never designed for developing or third-world or pre-industrial countries unless they could handle the inevitable complexity of mixed economies, the diversity, non-tribalism and essential human rights agenda of cosmopolitanism, and the rule of law. Those non-Western countries that have managed to hoist themselves into what is now a collapsing global system have accepted the hegemony of the Bretton Woods social contract.

45 Remarks at Opening Plenary UN Global Compact Leaders Forum by John G. Ruggie, Harvard University, Former UN Special Representative for Business and Human Rights, New York, 20 September 2013; www.hks.harvard.edu/m-rcbg/CSRI/RuggieGCOpeningPlenarySept2013.pdf, accessed 27 November 2014.
46 In the 1960s Marshall McLuhan predicted, in various publications, that the internet would become a form of global consciousness, and therefore one connected village. He was just a few decades ahead of the fact, but much of what he had to say is worth revisiting.

These countries already include Japan, Singapore, Taiwan and South Korea, while other countries that scramble to board the ship – without many of the fundamentals such as the rule of law or democracy – like India, China, Brazil, Indonesia, Russia and Nigeria – struggle to contain and defeat tribalism, misogyny, corruption, gross wealth inequality and provide a basic welfare, healthcare system and symbolic or totemic freedom of speech.

Francis Fukuyama has pointed out in his updated paean of praise to neoliberalism *The End of History and The Last Man*, called *Political Order and Political Decay*, that the hegemonic desire to impose democracy fails where there is no strong state. So, Japan in 1945 worked but Iraq and Afghanistan in the late twentieth century failed; George W. Bush, Donald Rumsfeld *et al.* failed to learn from emperor MacArthur in Japan. Any transparency associated with a liberating internet will lead to new forms of global governance, perhaps dominated by Orwellian surveillance and megadata capture by governments and corporations.

Way before the birth of Facebook, Twitter or Instagram, but at the dawn of multi-media reality via radio, television, telephones and computers, psychologist Kenneth Gergen said that being bombarded with multiple images and flooded with data and submerged in incoherence challenged the idea of identity, while at the same time enlarging our consciousness and connecting as never before. But, most fundamentally, to understand mind and consciousness is to understand that the brain is merely an engine for amalgamating numerous messages from everywhere. But now, because so much of that messaging or stimulus is coming to us through cognate sensing, we know too much or are aware too much of the mass of stimulus coming our way – and we are confused. Gergen referred to this as 'the

Saturated Self'.[47] The old way – modernism – distinguished things, categorised ideas, and neatly put everything from ideas to subjects to objects into boxes. But, as Gergen says, 'as one increasingly becomes aware of multiplicity in perspective, things in themselves disappear from view'.[48]

One of the leaflets at the New York Occupy (OWS) site said that it was social media that started the process and 'it is social media that can be used to create the new, socially oriented, human mindset'. A Dawkins meme was released (or is that given birth to?) on 13th July 2011 by an anarchistically minded anthropologist David Graeber who posted the provocation through adbusters: 'Occupy Wall Street, bring a tent' accompanied by a picture of a ballet dancer on top of the Wall Street bull. And they did, first in New York and then all over the world.[49] Graeber also coined the slogan 'we are the 99%' and it is around such simple expressions that ideas and people can rally. Who doesn't recognise and align with the idea?

Of course, Wall Street and the London Stock Exchange, the sites of two Occupy encampments, were simply symbolic, meant to highlight places where people, mostly energetic men – more on that in Chapter 3 – meet to engage in the sharp end of capitalism: trading in stocks and shares and swapping currencies for currencies. They are the most real symbols of the current system, but what they represent is illusory; it is everywhere and nowhere, for we are all embedded in it and our everyday lives are increasingly hostage to its apparent freedom and morality. If the demonstrators thought they were speaking

47 Kenneth J. Gergen, *The Saturated Self: Dilemmas of Identity in Contemporary Life* (New York: Basic Books, 1991).
48 Gergen, *The Saturated Self*: 112.
49 David Graeber, *The Democracy Project: A History, a Crisis, a Movement* (London: Allen Lane, 2013).

truth to power, which they were, they should remember that power normally knows the truth because that is how it gained so much – power and, today, so much wealth.

The media, as I have said, wanted to know what the protestors were calling for – what is the grand idea? But this time, unlike demonstrations in the 1930s in Europe and the USA for votes, civil rights and for employment, and unlike demonstrations for civil rights and against the Vietnam War in the 1960s, these demonstrations were about much more. This time, post-capitalism, post-communism, pre-sustainability, and amidst climate change, the action was concerned with a universal call for accountability by global institutions and for the age of globality.

In this fertile space, dangerous-philosopher Slavoj Žižek, speaking to the Occupy crowd in London outside St Paul's Cathedral, articulated the general idea across all Occupy sites, and presaged many of the demonstrations against dictators and corrupt totalitarian governments in the Middle East and Asia, when he said: 'We are allowed to think about alternatives.'[50] Graeber said that the Occupy movement was prefigurative, meaning that it was about the possibilities that might be possible in a freer environment, particularly a world that had not been co-opted by a corrupt form of finance-based capitalism.

The work of Swilling and others, cited earlier, shows that rapid evolutions in society take at least forty years to be enacted. So, some forty years or so after the civil rights movement in the US, and a similar period after street action across Europe associated with the broad and beautifully-floaty-but-vague aspirations of love, peace and happiness, we have seen

---

50 Reported in *The Guardian*, 24 October 2011 (letters page): 31.

advances in political freedom which have built on centuries of emancipation and inclusion.

And, not to be dismissed too lightly, in the post-60s, post-European decolonisation of much of Africa and other parts of the world, according to the UN more than 60% of the world's peoples live in nominally democratic states – even if Graeber thinks that democracy has been co-opted.[51] Let's think about the idea of living in a post-democratic world, a world dominated by social media, connectivity, globality and all the problems that ensue from that conception and practice. As two of the OccupyLSX (Occupy the London Stock Exchange) movement said, the 99% need to stop seeing themselves just as consumers (they obviously are, we all are) and become participants (we all are, but need to be more so): with 'systemic failure . . . we're in the business of describing [the] process' by which we will not just 'think about a new system . . . but start making one . . . [it's] about the way we, as individuals, understand democracy'.[52]

Walking through the Occupy sites, as I voyeuristically did, ignoring the Occupy New York handwritten poster to 'stop taking photos and join us', it was clear that the core of unhappy campers were making common union with often very disparate ideas but with that one big question: 'how is it that we have a financial collapse, a credit crunch, and how come the system can suddenly from nowhere produce vast bundles of bailout cash when it couldn't provide a living minimum wage in the

---

51 United Nations Development Programme, Human Development Reports; hdr.undp.org/en/data.

52 Naomi Colvin and Kai Wargalla, 'What we're really doing at St Paul's', *The Guardian*, 23 October 2011; www.theguardian.com/commentisfree/2011/oct/23/way-forward-99-occupy-london, accessed 14 December 2014.

US and the UK, or when thousands of people are losing their homes across the world because of the credit restrictions?'

While Occupiers were of all ages and from all backgrounds (OK, they were joined by the dispossessed wherever Occupy was established, looking for food and comfort; and in New York the dispossessed were dumped there by the City authorities to disrupt the camps), they were of a new global breed, a cosmopolitan set used to eating sushi, curry and avocados right through the year. They were used to being saturated by global images, to use Gergen's depiction of modern life in post-industrial society. They had heard the call on their hand-held devices.

To use the generational categories invented by the media and advertising industries, this lot were a mixture of four groups: the Pre-war generation (WWII), Baby Boomers, Generation X, all with the attitudes of neoliberal capitalism of consumerism, individualism and globality in Generation Y. This generation were born into rising prosperity in the West, and have now found that austerity is the name of the game; and they are increasingly finding that the idea of 'public' has been replaced by 'private' and the commoditisation of everything. But they care about issues often outside local borders: issues that transcend state boundaries, such as the environment, resource depletion and ethical sourcing. This group do not see difference in people, they see diversity and largely accept it; they expect information to be free and readily available, and are often globally travelled. Through the internet they share ideas with people they have often never met but are part of effective communities, or affinity networks.

This lot are also all part of the debt-generation, whatever their age. In the post-1979 bank boom created by Margaret Thatcher and Ronald Reagan's model of financial deregulation, everyone borrowed like there was no tomorrow with debts often secured against spuriously rapidly increasing property values. I remember well one day in the 1990s being told that we had notionally become millionaires as our house was now worth twice what we thought! Deluded, I too borrowed too much . . . and then when we sold we had lost almost as much as we had apparently gained.

Michael Lewis's *The Big Short* and *Boomerang* offer four revelations on the credit collapse in 2008/9: one, that it was relatively easy to find people who had made a fortune betting this would happen; two, that it revealed cultural stereotypes – the Germans didn't play (they didn't get into personal or national debt), the Americans bought big houses, Icelanders became bankers and stopped being fishers, and the British went shopping for houses, cars, holidays and shoes; three, that credit and debt were seen as real money, not credit or debt; four, that this money meant temptations could be satisfied, rather like during wars for partying soldiers when it comes to sex and alcohol – forget the consequences.[53]

In apologia for the way financial institutions had played the hard-working public for all they could make, and in the process made many bankers rich beyond most people's wildest dreams, the then CEO of Barclays Bank, Bob Diamond, made several contradictory remarks. He said that free-market Chicago economist Milton Friedman was one his favourites, then he said he disagreed with Friedman that the sole social purpose of business is to increase profits. Diamond said: 'Businesses must increase profits in a way that creates sustainable

---

53 Michael Lewis, *The Big Short: Inside the Doomsday Machine* (London: Penguin, 2011); *Boomerang: The Meltdown Tour* (London: Penguin, 2011).

shareholder value, not just short-term gain'.[54] This statement challenges the whole edifice of the financial services industry and the structure of global capitalism as it now stands, which is not to deny that some industries have to make long-term strategic investment decisions but accepts that they do so against the background of a rampant worldwide debt industry where global debt looking for a return jumped from $84 billion in 2002 to about $200 billion eight years later.

Chapter 4 of this book looks at the underlying structures that govern our dominant global organisations and institutions; but meanwhile the situation was summed up by a former chairman of Lazard's, and now a professor of commerce, who, like me, spent time at the OccupyLSX camp outside St Paul's Cathedral. His simple observation, which I echo, is that Adam Smith, who is often quoted in support of free markets, thought he was talking about morality when he talked about the market economy. He argued that such a market, as in the first sense of buying a kilo of apples or a length of cloth from a stall holder, was based on trust, respect and integrity, and it is these virtues that no longer drive capitalism. Professor Ken Costa, a former senior manager at bankers UBS, says that thinking, writing and talking about values and ethics will be 'like learning an entirely new language' for many people in business.[55]

So much of the way the modern world is ordered finds its origin in the birth of the industrial revolution 250 years ago and the European colonisation of the world more than 400

54 Bob Diamond, 'Today Business Lecture 2011', BBC; news.bbc. co.uk/today/hi/today/newsid_9630000/9630673.stm, accessed 5 March 2014.

55 Ken Costa, 'Why the city should heed the discordant voices of St Paul's', *Financial Times*, 28 October 2011; on.ft.com/1GiozKT, accessed 5 March 2014.

years ago. Take, for example, IBM who want to be perceived as being at the cutting edge of the current slow-moving evolution of marrying people and planet, a marriage made in heaven or in the 1960s: 'business was the driving force of the industrial revolution, the guiding force behind the digital revolution and must now become the leading force in the sustainability revolution'.[56] This slightly oversimplified version of the past, present and future leaves out the reckoning that we now live in an age of multiplicity, complex social networks and converging paradigms. It is not possible to argue that public or private policy now dominates, but it is possible to argue that marketisation, commoditisation and consumption are the distinctive characteristics of the global economy. What remains is to wrest these characteristics to work in favour of people and planet and not just the 1%. I believe we are on the way.

Too little is made in political discussion of art, satire and humour as tools of expression and release. Russia may have tried to incarcerate the all-female rock band Pussy Riot in the 2010s with much sarcastic global laughter. Jokes often cut to the bone more effectively than slogans, political commentary or scholarly disquisitions. A carton can change the world as much as a thousand words. Woody Guthrie's guitar was inscribed with the line 'this machine kills fascists'. The thirtieth-anniversary annual humour exhibition in Brazil held in 2012 said that 'humor [is] the gift of discerning and exposing the clay feet of false earthly gods, the courage to "roast" the arrogant . . . Even in their lowest moments – in a cell or a slave's quarters – human beings are laughing creatures . . . oppressors know what to do

56 Ibm.com/uk/start, November 2011.

against weapons but when faced with a joke that cuts to the bone . . .'.[57]

In Zuccotti Square, New York, someone had parked a large white van displaying the words: 'WikiLeaks: TOP SECRET'. In New York and London the slogans were: 'The Beginning is Nigh!', 'Tahrir Square, EC4M, City of Westminster', 'Eat The Rich',[58] and possibilities for discussion: 'Separation of Corporation and State', 'a living minimum wage and a maximum wage', 'we know the problem, can we find a solution?', 'WE occupy'. In New York, Abraham Lincoln was popular: 'America will never be destroyed from the outside. If we falter and lose our freedoms, it will be because we destroyed ourselves.' In London the 1647 Putney Debates were quoted: 'I think the poorest he that is in England, has a life to live as the greatest he.' At all sites there were libraries of donated books from all points of view, courses being taught under canvas, and very vigorous debates taking place. These were sites of discussion, knowledge sharing, bigotry and sharing, laughter and anger which became tourist sites and media havens. As a former BBC journalist, I know what you need most for television news is pictures of the revolution taking place: so burn a tyre, climb a statue, smash up a McDonald's, camp outside a cathedral, or occupy a public square and we'll be there. The pictures will go viral and global instantaneously. An internet revolution is so much harder to capture. Action can speak louder than a million tweets.

---

57 *Ícaro, Brazil: Revista de Bordo VARIG* (*VARIG Inflight Magazine*) 239 (July 2004); www.varig-airlines.com/en/icarobrasil.htm.
58 A reference by an eighteen-year-old to P.J. O'Rourke's 1998 *Eat The Rich* (Picador). She had travelled across the USA from her home in Wyoming to be part of the Occupy event in New York.

The post-colonial gaze

The way we see the world counts for how globality and Earth awareness develops. Europe may have developed in leaps and bounds since the end of two internal wars that became world wars in the first half of the twentieth century, but for the world that was colonised and brutalised by Europe for a couple of centuries prior to the twentieth the anger of suppression is still bubbling. The USA carries on where Europeans left off in a largely unrecognised proxy arrangement promoting all the baggage of the civilised state: the rule of law, human rights, representative government, freedom of expression and that greatest of all Euro-American exports: democracy. But this exported democracy package has embedded within it a model of capitalism, a model of markets, a model of property rights, and many cultural assumptions that defy the traditions of the countries that are supposed to import it wholesale. It took Europeans, and its disciples the USA, Canada, Australia and New Zealand, centuries to arrive at this cultural model, not least because they suffered at their own hands particularly during the First and Second World Wars. Now we expect others to adopt our ways and means wholesale in a generation or two, such is our myopia, forgetfulness and arrogance.

The post-colonial gaze sees Europeans looking past their own colonial mistakes as they have moved on. It sees Americans viewing the world as their fiefdom for business, development and militarisation – all in a good cause, of course: namely, world peace, human rights and democracy. But for much of the rest of the world the centuries of oppression and colonisation have yet to be reversed.

Major Watkin Tench, was in charge of one of the first fleet ships as part of the invasion of Australia by the UK in 1788.

The quote below expresses the pioneering spirit of British expansionism. It's a beautifully written piece, but, to all intents and purposes, it sees Australia as *terra nullius* – an empty land, devoid of human habitation and belonging to no one. If there were Indigenous people, they were not urbanised so under international law, as it was then, they were not owners; and, under the model of governance being exported, settlement and buildings denoted ownership while nomadism and careful stewardship were not recognised as civilisation.

> Here we paused, surveying the 'wild abyss: pondering our voyage'. Before us lay the trackless immeasurable desert, in awful silence. At length, after consultation, we determined to steer west and by north, by compass, the make of the land in that quarter indicating the existence of a river. We continued to march all day through a country untrodden by European foot. Save that a melancholy crow now and then flew overhead, or a kangaroo was seen to bound at a distance, the picture of solitude was complete and undisturbed.[59]

The colonial gaze is also well captured by William Golding's 1954 book, which later became an award-winning film, *Lord of the Flies*:

> We've got to have rules and obey them. After all, we're not savages. We're English, and the English are best at everything.[60]

---

59 Watkin Tench, *1788* (Melbourne: Text Publishing, 1789, 2009): 111. 'Wild abyss' is taken from John Milton, *Paradise Lost*, II: 917.

60 William Golding, *Lord of the Flies* (London: Penguin Modern Classics, 1954): 42.

There isn't the space in this essay to look at the other side of globality: that is, for many people the fruits of international trade, growing globalism and globalisation have not been wonderful harvests. They have left some one-third of the world without security, without clean water and healthcare systems, with corrupt leaders and totalitarian systems that care not a jot for citizenship or engagement with human rights and the rule of law. It is very difficult for people in what is known as 'the West' to understand the post-colonial gaze, and the abiding resentment at being derided for so long, at having their customs and religions ignored. This is as true of China, which will not be bullied, as it is of Japan, which will continue to 'Japanise' any Western influence, as it is of India, which utilises democracy in a completely different way from the USA or Britain, and most of the Middle East (which is itself a colonial term), which cannot shake off the burden of oppressive government, or Brazil, whose class system maintains the grossly unequal distribution of wealth that is the result of Portuguese, Spanish, French and British empire builders. To expect these countries to embrace democracy and free and fair markets when they have never experienced them is to expect too much too quickly.

It is not that I want to support the oppression of women in the Middle East, the gross inequalities of Brazil or South Africa, or the military dictatorships that spring up across Asia. But I do want Europeans and Americans to recognise the post-colonial gaze: to see the mote in their eye, to not throw stones in glass houses. The world is as it is because of the way it was. Trade arrangements, pollution levels, wealth accumulation and attitudes are set because particularly Europeans exploited the rest of the world, usually from behind the barrel of a gun, over many centuries. It should be no surprise that post-colonial countries are now exposing their wounds.

Edward Said's thinking on post-colonialism divides the world into ways of seeing the world, which hint at geographical areas but are more states of mind. So, for him, the world is divided between the Orient and the Occident, the latter having had the power to oppress in the last few hundreds of years and is now challenged by having to recognise 'the other', an other, a different way of seeing everything – particularly history.[61]

But while we contemplate the other side of waves of globalisation that have delivered the world as it is today, the madman also stands at the gates of dawn. However much we may want to move smoothly between the dystopia of industrial capitalism to a new utopia of care, sufficiency and resilience, the fact is that one madman with a bomb can ruin your day. The short- to medium-term threat to our prosperity and survival lies in failing to adapt to climate change or rebuilding global capitalism; but an immediate threat is posed by the possibility of nuclear conflagration.

Nuclear weaponry brings immediate suicide, while a failure to adapt to climate change brings a slow suicide – a slide into chaos and irretrievable end points.

The upsides of an interdependent, neurally connected world are many, but the downside brings with it the possibility that a few rogue men with a single warhead and a delivery method could threaten all our local projects and grand narratives. However, the upside of this world is that we may now know we are one world and act fast enough to evolve and adapt to a post-climate-change future. But this requires significant

61 For more on the post-colonial gaze, see Pankaj Mishra, *From the Ruins of Empire: The Revolt Against the West and the Remaking of Asia* (London: Penguin, 2012) or Edward W. Said, *Orientalism* (London: Vintage, 1979).

systems changes to our organising principles, particularly in relation to capitalism and corporations.

In the meantime, 'the quadrennial celebration of the spring-time of humanity' (the Olympic Games) and other global events and celebrations allow us to believe that it is possible to continue our progress towards a new world.

2

Rebalancing science and awe

In Chapter 1 I said that globality and Earth awareness is the dominant leitmotif of the twenty-first century. It was given vision and clarity by Anders's photograph of Earthrise on 24th December 1968 coming round from the dark side of the Moon. The technology of the two world wars in the first half of the twentieth century highlighted the sense of place – the place and space we all share – that was not possible previously. The First and Second World Wars are not only turning points in understanding man's use of technology in the pursuit of inhumanity to man, but also in understanding the idea of shared space and our place in it. Now that this sense is compounded by our growing understanding of Earth systems science, and particularly climate change science, the question 'What does it mean to be human now that we know what we know?' is both qualitatively and quantitatively different in this century.

The question is different now from the timeless screaming at the universe for answers to the inexplicable. It is supremely arrogant and self-serving to expect to know or fully understand everything. The idea that we might think we know our state may be satisfying and help us sleep better, but in the long run it is a deceit. If this makes me a denier of the climate change science, then so be it. But I am not a denier of the science as it now stands, and this is a subtle but vast difference between me and those who religiously deny science per se. These denialists are denying the truth of scientific storytelling. That is not tenable.

There are many examples of the straightforward denial of knowledge for the sake of the mental glue of religious fundamentalism. One extreme example comes from a medical doctor, who presumably uses science to diagnose his patients:

> All that stuff I was taught about evolution and embryology and the Big Bang Theory, all that is lies straight from the pit of Hell. And it's lies to try and keep me and all the folks who were taught that from understanding that they need a saviour.

In 2014 Paul Broun was a medical doctor and Congressman in the USA.[1]

But, as the scientist and mathematician Jacob Bronowski said in 1973,

> Dream or nightmare, we have to live our experience as it is, and we have to live it awake. We live in a world which is penetrated through and through by science and which is both whole and real. We cannot turn it into a game simply by taking sides.[2]

1 https://broun.house.gov, accessed 29 October 2014 and other dates previously.
2 Jacob Bronowski quoted in Lawrence M. Krauss, *A Universe from Nothing: Why There Is Something Rather Than Nothing* (New York: Free Press, 2012): 181.

Bronowski's mammoth television series *The Ascent of Man* echoed Charles Darwin's *The Descent of Man* and Kenneth Clarke's *Civilisation*, with Bronowski arguing strongly for both the scientific falsifiability test *and* a developed sense of awe and wonder.

In Shakespeare's *Hamlet* being is conflated with not-being, in the most quoted speech on the meaning of life, 'to be or not to be', so that the two, the quick and the dead, are perceived as two sides of the same coin; without one we cannot know the other. This metaphysics rests well with another of Shakespeare's plays, *All's Well That Ends Well*, when he talks of 'The web of our life is a mingled yarn, good and ill together.' The idea that life is a continuing story, or yarn, where the endeavour is to understand it through storytelling – using metaphor and analogy, mixing ideas of right and wrong, good and evil, fact and fiction – seems to me to be a more useful way to begin to understand the question posed here, 'What does it mean to be human now that we know what we know?' Knowing and not-knowing are of a piece, just as *understanding* science and *believing* in mystery are part and parcel of the whole. This chapter is entitled 'Rebalancing science and awe', and part of this rebalancing is a re-recognition of narrative. All written, spoken, musical, acted, artistic forms are narrative, however hard some scientists and economists may try to deny the values their analyses are based on. Figures may tell us something and are often very important, but they don't speak to us. Julian Barnes, the Booker Prize-winning novelist, says that:

> Fiction, more than any other written form, explains and expands life. Biology, of course, also explains life; so do biography and biochemistry and biophysics and biomechanics and biopsychology. But all the biosciences yield to fiction. Novels tell us

the most truth about life: what it is, how we live
it, what it might be for, how we enjoy and value
it, how it goes wrong, and how we lose it. Novels speak to and from the mind, the heart, the
eye, the genitals, the skin; the conscious and the
unconscious.[3]

Doesn't every age think it is special? I take that charge on
the chin. But I do believe that, because of what we now know
about the state of the planet and our history, and have known
for over a half a century, the paradigm is genuinely shifting
and we need a new narrative that takes in the stories of the
silent, and a narrative that rebalances science and awe – what
we know, what we don't know, what we know we don't know,
and, most important, what we don't know we don't know.
That is awe: mystery. The *unknown* unknown.

Martin Rees, former president of the Royal Society and eminent cosmologist, has said emphatically that 'we have entered
an era when human beings pose a greater threat than nature
to the earth's future'.[4] Others have joined him, such as Clive
Hamilton in *Requiem for a Species*, who said that 'as the climate crisis unfolds, and poses the question of the future of
humankind, the meaning of our lives will come increasingly to
the fore'.[5]

In *Living in the End Times*, philosopher Slavoj Žižek claims
we are living through a period where we are in denial that
an apocalypse is possible, but when it comes we will see it as

3 Julian Barnes, *Through the Window: Seventeen Essays (and One
Short Story)* (London: Vintage, 2012): Preface.
4 Martin Rees, 'Are we all doomed?', *New Statesman*, 6 June 2011:
23.
5 Clive Hamilton, *Requiem for a Species: Why We Resist the Truth
about Climate Change* (London: Earthscan, 2010): 219.

normal. I am very sympathetic to his view that this is a moment in human history of revelation, a liberating moment, when if we look hard enough we can evolve to a higher level of consciousness because we will understand our absolute dependence not on the arrogance and aggressivity of the current model of exploitative capitalism but on an Earth-centric model of development that respects natural limits. So, this is the moment where he says, paradoxically, 'we should alienate ourselves more from nature to be aware of our fragility'. He says that he has 'a very naïve Enlightenment fascination with science . . . but the era of relativism, where science was just another product of knowledge, is ending. We philosophers should be asking those big metaphysical questions about quantum physics, about "reality" and working with physicists and the like on questions such as "what is the meaning of life? What is reality? What is consciousness?" '[6]

It is very important to note that, in transdisciplinary teams, or indeed in trying to reach across intellectual boundaries (and proverbially 'think outside the box'), there has to be a high level of trust. I have to trust my climate change colleagues when they explain the apocalyptic state of the world's climate and what seems like a high possibility of a more than 2° rise in average global temperatures. That trust is built through my affection for these people, and through my engagement with their discourse: I must trust yet be sceptical and enquiring at the same time.

Language, Žižek suggests, is incomplete as a way of answering these questions, and we will only know this when we come to appreciate its incompleteness. In other words, it is impossible to answer these questions – but we are desperate to have

6 Žižek, *Living in the End Times*; see also Slavoj Žižek, 'Wake Up and Smell the Apocalypse', *New Scientist*, 28 August 2010: 28.

answers in a science-crazy, objectified world. In the end, we will always be incomplete. And, in the long run, as John Maynard Keynes said, 'we are all dead'. Or, through the power of thought, we human beings can make statements about what the world will be like in a while – or a trillion years. String theorist Brian Greene finds this exciting. 'This erases any fear of doom,'[7] he says.

As I said in the Introduction, it is possible to believe that humans are a brief experiment and that we will not survive. Crispin Tickell, the author of Margaret Thatcher's radical climate change speech to the UN General Assembly in 1989, has similarly expressed these thoughts: when you look at human history and the evolution of the cosmos and the current state of climate change science, it is possible to argue that humankind has only a small chance of continuing for much longer. We are a soft-skinned animal that can survive only within a limited temperature range. Unless, perhaps, we clone with computers – but even then we forget our evolutionary past at our peril.

Yarning and storytelling

As a soft-skinned animal that can only survive within a limited temperature range, I am only really complete when I'm lying on my back in the grass listening to the skylarks and wondering. There is a bend in the road between East Portlemouth and Rickham in the South Hams of Devon, England, and the skylarks are sweeter at this point, overlooking the sea across the waving golden cornfields, than anywhere else on the planet.

7 Brian Greene, 'Are we all doomed?', New Statesman, 6 June 2011: 25.

While I want to believe the completeness of the current knowledge on climate change and the coming apocalypse, ironically this coming crisis is a moment of enlightenment that takes me to a higher level of consciousness, partly because I cannot comprehend it. I am liberated by my stupidity, or my not-knowingness.

There are two grounds for questioning the current scientific consensus on climate change – and consensus it is – but there are no grounds for outright denial: outright denial seems to be a dysfunctional personality predisposition. The first basis for questioning is that of logical scepticism and enquiry: can I ever, as a generalist, fully comprehend the enormity of what I am being told, or is it always going to be a question of belief on my part in my colleagues and in the scientific method? The second is that science, or that which is perceived as the current truth, is but one part of the whole story, and that in yarning more and better I will be able to share not only what is apparently known but also have some sense of how my fellow humans see the situation so that we can share our lives and experience.

The Bible, the Quran, the Vedas and other fundamental religious texts are but stories liberally mixed with some truth-telling about human nature and all its marvels. It has often been commented that if you were to find yourself alone forever on a deserted island (perhaps a desert island) and wanted stories that told universal truths without any recourse to the glue of faith or fundamentalism, then taking Shakespeare's collected works would serve you better than a religious text. Shakespeare would give you colour, songs to sing, and some great jokes! If one took the IPCC's reports, on the grounds that there is enough detail to keep you busy till the ends of your days, you would probably want to commit suicide because the underlying rationality is so depressing. There are no jokes in IPCC reports or the Bible. What we need is to be absolved in art, in metaphor, in humour, in 'The web of our life . . . [in] mingled yarn, good and ill together', as Shakespeare says.

Gro Harlem Brundtland, the chair of the 1987 report *Our Common Future* – which gave the world the standard definition of sustainable development, which is so often quoted (not least by students wanting to start an essay somewhere and businesses anxious to be seen as environmentally literate) – also said in 2012 that 'our generation is the first to understand the risks facing humanity. We must act decisively.'[8] *Our Common Future* was also the first major international report to nod in the direction of the web of life, to see the complex interrelations between people and planet, between all organic and inorganic matter, and between spirituality and the way we live.

Prior to Rio+20, the Earth Summit held in Rio de Janeiro in June 2012, the UN High Level Panel on Global Sustainability (whose members included Gro Harlem Brundtland) published a report entitled *Resilient People, Resilient Planet*. Here they said that there is a need for 'a new political economy' for sustainable development which brings together those people who for 'too long have talked past each other – economists, social activists and environmental scientists . . . speaking different languages, or at least different dialects'.[9]

The idea that we have choice is common to UN reports, and to many of those who believe in willpower and hope, which I do. I also err on the side of the line that 'life is what happens to you while you're busy making other plans' (a favourite of Buddhists and often attributed to John Lennon's 1980 song

8 Brundtland, 'Earth Agonistes'.
9 United Nations Secretary-General's High-Level Panel on Global Sustainability, *Resilient People, Resilient Planet*: 12.

'Beautiful Boy', although he was not the first to use it). Developing a sustainable enterprise economy is a never-ending journey, like stepping into a fast-flowing river, and this metaphoric discourse is commonplace in the literature on sustainability. In *Resilient People, Resilient Planet* it says 'sustainable development is not a destination, but a dynamic process of adaptation, learning and action. It is about recognizing, understanding and acting on interconnections – above all on those between economy, society and the natural environment'.[10] This, then is the web of life – the interconnections.

When asked, commentators as seemingly diverse as David Attenborough and Richard Dawkins say that the one bit of science that everyone should know about is 'the unity of life', meaning the web of complexity and interconnectedness of life. Richard Dawkins, Martin Rees and others clarify this by saying that there needs to be a greater understanding of the unity of life on Earth which has come about through evolution and natural selection. Dawkins says that 'we are the only species capable of understanding it [unity, systems and webs]' which is, I think, stretching our capacity a little and I would qualify this by saying 'capable of endeavouring to understand'. We are the only species on Earth capable of thinking we have understood what goes on around us and then acting on that knowledge. There should be rather more trepidation about our certainty, and a whole lot more awe for what we cannot understand.

But at this point I'm lying on my back in the long grass listening to the skylarks above me on a summer's day, being here now and not so concerned with what might be lurking. Dawkins sees the issue as one of human consciousness: are we capable of knowing, or how are we capable of knowing? The

10 Ibid.

theoretical physicist and cosmologist Stephen Hawking says that to fully understand evolution in nature is to understand and recognise that evolution pays no respect to social justice and that it is as disregarding to Homo sapiens as it is to all the other species that have ever lived on Earth. In other words, to understand the flowing river that is evolution is to understand that we have no God-given right to expect to continue. Extinction is the norm, not an aberration or something that humans through their management or mismanagement of the Earth have suddenly invented.

To be conscious of this idea is to be conscious of the idea of being and not being, for, just as our own lives are transient and impermanent ('we're all going to die'), so too is human life on Earth. That we are conscious of being alive does not necessarily give us a right to continue being around to be conscious of our existence. But Stephen Hawking says we are near to knowing 'the theory of everything' and that the discovery of the Higgs boson particle, or the 'god particle' as it is sometimes called, is one of the missing links. Like most of my readers I pretend to be capable of fully understanding these matters but it would be arrogant of me to say I fully comprehend. I can only hope that the yarn, or story, Hawking and others are telling me has some validity as far as it goes.

This is important because the same is true when it comes to dealing with the science of everyday life, and in particular with the notion of 'the end times' or 'the requiem for the species' or 'man's last century', defined by the climate change hypothesis and discussed by philosophers like Slavoj Žižek and Clive Hamilton and cosmologists like Martin Rees.

The physicist Brian Cox says we know that the universe began with the Big Bang 13.8 billion years ago, that our solar system started life 4.6 billion years ago and that there are 100 billion stars in our Milky Way galaxy. He knows he knows until it is refuted or science evolves to tell us the next story. This is Karl Popper's falsifiability test, but it is only theoretically testable, empirical evidence in this area being difficult to obtain.

Albert Einstein told us that time and space are continuous and contiguous, but we have since discovered that neither are as synchronous as Einstein thought. He wasn't wrong; there has just been further knowledge added to his original outrageous thinking. As Martin Rees says, 'we don't know what banged in The Big Bang and why it banged'. The question for Rees, which is of fascination to me, is whether we are capable of understanding what we are talking about:

> Will we ever be able to understand our cosmos and the complexities within it ... What's important and interesting is the pattern and structure – the emergent complexity ... the Grand Design has no relevance to most of the things that humans value ... perhaps our brains don't have enough conceptual grasp.[11]

Quiet leadership and science and awe

When those who work on the paradigm shift that is real sustainable development are asked what their most formative influences have been, they often put two authors near the top of their thoughts: Rachel Carson and Fritjof Capra. They were

11 Martin Rees, 'Even the theory of everything has limits', *The Telegraph* (UK), 19–25 September 2012: 26.

both eminent and rigorous scientists who could also spin a yarn. Rachel Carson was a US toxicologist and Fritjof Capra trained as a nuclear physicist. Carson is best known for her 1962 book *Silent Spring* and Capra's most cited book is *The Turning Point*, published in 1982. (Thirty-two years later, in 2014, he published *The Systems View of Life*.)

Margaret Atwood, the award-winning Canadian novelist, says that 'Rachel Carson is a saint' because all Carson called for was sound science and the precautionary principle and she denied those who wanted to promote social Darwinism: 'Carson questioned this dualism. Whatever airs we might give ourselves, "we" [are] not distinct from "it": we [are] part of it, and [can] live only inside it. To think otherwise was self-destructive.'[12]

Silent Spring changed the way we see the relationship between people and planet. As a professional toxicologist she applied a razor-sharp mind to the links between the decline in bird life and the increased use of pesticides in farming. As a writer she wrote beautiful and inspiring prose. The opening lines of *Silent Spring* could be the opening scene of a Hollywood film script:

> There was once a town in the heart of America where all life seemed to live in harmony with its surroundings. The town lay in the midst of a checkerboard of prosperous farms, with fields of grain and hillsides of orchards where, in spring, white clouds of bloom drifted above the green fields ... Then a strange blight crept over the area ... What has silenced the voices of spring in countless towns in America?

12 Margaret Atwood, 'Rachel Carson's Silent Spring, 50 years on', *The Guardian*, 7 December 2012; www.theguardian.com/books/2012/dec/07/why-rachel-carson-is-a-saint, accessed 1 December 2014.

The backlash against her work was furious, particularly from chemical companies and those with vested interests. In retrospect, it resembles the backlash against the anti-slavery movement in the eighteenth and nineteenth centuries; the lies and deceit of the tobacco industry in the twentieth century; the lies, denials and abnegation of social responsibility by the processed food sector today; and the fossil fuel industry's deceit and obfuscation in the twenty-first century.

If it sounds familiar, it is: she was accused of being a 'bunny hugger' who would drag society and technological progress back to the middle ages. And yet she never advocated banning chemicals or pesticides, just that they should be properly tested and their use managed carefully. She said that they were being sold to farmers by men who did not fully understand what they were selling. This is similar to those sales people who sold prime-rate mortgages to people who could not afford them in the last few decades. Her crime was apparently compounded by being a woman, and a woman who was a scientist. How could a woman be scientifically analytical and detached – surely she would be emotional and irrational? US President Eisenhower was advised that she was 'probably a communist' and her mental state was questioned because she was unmarried and had no children.[13]

Fritjof Capra trained in theoretical high-energy physics. *Turning Point* is subtitled *Science, Society and the Rising Culture* and argues for an holistic, systems-based approach

---

13 Ezra Taft Benson, a former US Agricultural Secretary of State, wrote in a private letter that because Carson was unmarried despite being attractive, she was 'probably a communist'. Mark Stoll, 'Rachel Carson's *Silent Spring*: A Book That Changed the World', 2012; www.environmentandsociety.org/exhibitions/silent-spring/personal-attacks-rachel-carson, accessed 4 August 2014.

to understanding life which mixes science and metascience. Capra, in tune with modern physics, wrote that 'ecological awareness will arise only when we combine our rational knowledge with an intuition for the nonlinear nature of our environment'. He points out that such wisdom, for this is wisdom rather than simply information or knowledge, is the basis of many Indigenous, traditional cultures around the world who have a 'refined awareness of the environment'.[14]

Our technological knowledge is high and leads onward and upwards, particularly when it comes to new consumer products and fast foods, but it continually divorces us from the planet that supports life on Earth. So it is that we reject the precautionary principle in favour of profit and scientific experimentation.

Business and management reading is stuffed with literature on leadership, but I want to promote the likes of Carson, Darwin, Capra and indeed Margaret Atwood as examples of quiet leadership as well as being the real heroes of sustainable development.

Reviving natural philosophy and promoting quiet leadership

I want to argue in favour of a return to what used to be called 'natural philosophy' where men and women moved easily between what is known, and can be contested, and what is meditative, philosophical and spiritual.

---

14 Fritjof Capra, *The Turning Point: Science, Society and the Rising Culture* (New York: Simon & Schuster, 1982): 25.

In 1882 the German philosopher Friedrich Nietzsche declared that 'God is dead' because he argued that Charles Darwin and other evolutionists had made progress a matter of selection rather than the product of some grand design of god or the like. In a sense he was arguing, early on, the thesis that history is dead, man has triumphed – and indeed his thinking that atheism is linked to liberalism was subsequently a foundation for fascism and Nazism. But this argument was to misunderstand science and evolutionary theory, and this misunderstanding is one of the reasons for this chapter. Darwin never said that biological evolution was the sole determinant of evolution per se, and he had said that there were other factors that give rise to the way humans have evolved. But they are still animals and subject to biological evolution and adaptation. Darwin also never used the expression 'the survival of the fittest'; this was constructed by a journalist seeking to over-paraphrase. Darwin did say: 'Organisms with superior adaptive characteristics tend to survive and pass on these qualities'. Darwin had talked about evolution, adaptation and learning: the most supreme of humanity's differentiators.

Charles Darwin's *On The Origin of Species* was published on 24th November 1859, when he was 50 and some 23 years after he arrived back from a five-year trip around the world on HMS *Beagle*, which had left Portsmouth just after Christmas in 1831. It is a side note to this essay, but it is difficult for most people to understand in the twenty-first century the strength of faith and trust of all crew members when ships left shores bound for they-knew-not-exactly-where, on the other side of the world. A visit to his home, Down House in Downe, Kent, is a trip back in time: you can walk his walk round the garden, sit in his seat and ponder, and wander about his potting sheds and talk to the successors of his own plants, and stand and stare at his desk – just as he left it.

The term *social Darwinism* is often used when discussing social, rather than natural, evolution, but on this he has perhaps been misrepresented. Just as he saw that humans had evolved from animals, and were still largely animals, through natural selection in the case of humans this had been through the development of culture and the use of intelligence, creativity, enterprise and collectivism to overcome difficulties and progress. If societies, and groups of individuals, had developed differently, this was not surprising if they had not been exposed to the same competition and environmental forces. His diaries, particularly when he was in Tierra del Fuego and Australia, are full of references to his insights on social issues. He was a social progressive for his time and particularly abhorred, and campaigned against, slavery, as did the Darwin family and his wife's family, the Wedgwoods of the famous pottery company.

From his writing on natural and social issues it may be reasonable to suggest that Darwin's evolutionary theory could be followed to its logical extension and mean that humans will naturally disappear by bringing about their own destruction. Only through the application – and triumph – of intelligence, creativity, enterprise and collectivism will we overcome the present difficulties and prosper, survive and progress. If, that is, we have not already overshot. This is what is postulated by Martin Rees, thought to be certain by James Lovelock and denied by some others – that we have already overshot.

It is an irony, not lost on Darwin, that his life was blighted by, and he died of, the very thing that he had revealed to the world. Life is a struggle and natural selection does best when there is competitive advantage which is gained by uniting superior aspects often through combining the strengths of differing groups. His family of Darwins and Wedgwoods made themselves vulnerable to diseases and madness through their constant inbreeding, just as the European Royal families have done in the last few centuries. His research was largely funded by the significant commercial wealth of these two families, as well as funding from the UK government Treasury, thus making a link between business, science and progress. He subsequently made money through the sales of his books, the first print of *Species* selling out the first run of 1,250 copies in a short period.

The issues that arise now, in the twenty-first century, are straightforward: is life on Earth unique or brought about by a specific set of circumstances that could be replicated anywhere in the universe? Is this life just a local manifestation? Could there be other forms of intelligent life elsewhere that do not look anything like this? And could there be forms of life that have been created by intelligent, conscious life, but are now mechanistic and unconscious in the sense of having no morality, by which is meant no concern for others, and no sense of social justice? And could human life continue as a race, following our demise, as a result of having released a form of other non-conscious life into space which can replicate and develop and expand? Are we the natural creators of our own destruction, and, if so, does it matter? Are these questions the answer to the question 'What does it mean to be human now that we know what we know?' And, is this what Darwin meant by his 1871 use of the term 'the descent of man'? He concluded in *On the Origin of Species* (a very accessible text even today):

> There is grandeur in this view of life, with its several powers, having been originally breathed into a few forms or into one; and that, whilst this planet has gone cycling on according to the fixed law of gravity, from so simple a beginning endless forms

most beautiful and most wonderful have been, and
are being, evolved.[15]

One of the most fascinating aspects of Darwin's life was that,
because of his upbringing and education, and because a culture of enquiry was prevalent among cultivated gentlemen of
the period, he crossed intellectual boundaries with ease. This
can be ascribed to the widespread belief that God had created
everything, the Enlightenment notwithstanding; so to wander
through science, mysticism and creativity evinced an enquiring
mind, not confusion. And hence my call to promote the idea of
natural philosophy today. It was partly because of the schism
that Darwin's ideas created, and the further deliberations of
reductionism of science, that we have lost this ability to wander, and wonder, about the links between science, creation and
consciousness.

It was J.R.R. Tolkien, the author of *Lord of the Rings,* who
said: 'those who wander and wonder are not necessarily lost'.
Eminent scientists from Galileo to Newton, to Einstein, to Rees
and Lovelock have had, and have, no trouble in musing on
these issues and arguing their intellectual indivisibility. Indeed,
great leaps in knowledge tend to arrive at moments when the
curtains go up and the mental glue melts. In other words, fundamentalism is, per se, mental glue. Unless we can continually question, yarn and probe, we are lost to absolutism and
mired in intellectual poverty.[16] Similarly, Turner prize-winner

15 Charles Darwin, *On Natural Selection* (excerpts from *On the Origin of Species*, ed. J.W. Burrow; Camberwell, VIC, Australia: Penguin Books, 2004 [1859]): 117.
16 Žižek, *Living in the End Times*; 'Wake Up and Smell the
Apocalypse'.

Grayson Perry says that inspiration arrives out of the corner of the eye.

So, let's finish this short section on Charles Darwin's theory of evolution and its contribution to the current enquiry on the meaning of life, and what it means to be human, with a quotation from *Species* that leads neatly into the next witness for the arguments in this book. Here is Darwin on metaphor:

> I use the term Struggle for Existence in a large and metaphorical sense, including dependence of one being on another, and including (which is more important) not only the life of the individual, but success in leaving progeny ... The struggle for existence inevitably follows from the high rate at which all organic beings tend to increase. Every being, which during its natural lifetime produces several eggs or seeds, must suffer destruction during some period of its life, and during some season or occasional year, otherwise, on the principle of geometrical increase, its numbers would quickly become so inordinately great that no country could support the product ... It is not the strongest species that survive, nor the most intelligent, but the ones most responsive to change. In the struggle for survival, the fittest win out at the expense of their rivals because they succeed in adapting themselves best to their environment. It is the ones that are lucky, or already have the right features that can be passed on to the next generation.[17]

17 Darwin, *On Natural Selection*: 1-2.

Metaphor and science

In 2006 the Geological Society awarded James Lovelock the Wollaston Medal, which had previously been won by Darwin. Like Charles Darwin, James Lovelock moved between different disciplines: Darwin changed his initial degree course, and Lovelock, having been unable to afford university, only gained his first degree as a result of evening classes at Birkbeck College in London while working in a photography firm by day. Also common to all the polymaths discussed in this essay, Lovelock has a nonconformist attitude and disinclination towards formal education, preferring to follow his own lines of enquiry. I sympathise; my formal education taught me little, while my extracurricular activities and out-of-the-classroom modality taught me most. It was Rachel Carson's heroine, Beatrix Potter (1866–1943) – mycologist, painter, business woman, co-founder of the UK's National Trust and author of *Peter Rabbit* – who said: 'Thank goodness I was never sent to school; it would have rubbed off some of the originality.'

In the 1960s as a family we used to collect James Lovelock's mother Nell from her home in Roehampton every Sunday morning and take her to attend the Quaker meeting for worship at Kingston Friends Meeting. She would give us a weekly update on her son James who had gone to work for NASA in the USA – 'to see if there is life on other planets'! I was eight years old when James Lovelock joined NASA and I can remember being interested, even if uncomprehending of the enormity of what I was hearing.

There is a strong link between Darwin, Lovelock and Adam Smith, whose economics are often misguidedly used as the theoretical basis for neoliberal economic theory. Smith's best friend and trustee, James Hutton, who pre-dated Darwin by

100 years, and Lovelock by 200 years, argued that Earth is a single living entity.[18] Hutton founded first the Edinburgh Geological Society and then the Geological Society in London, which subsequently made awards to Darwin and Lovelock for their work on unified theory.

Lovelock's Gaia hypothesis, now a theory, says that the Earth is a massive self-regulating, living entity. The use of the name of the Greek goddess Gaia came about through a conversation with his friend and neighbour, novelist William Golding but Lovelock insists it is metaphorical language and needs to be thought of as such in order to rebut new-ageist connotations. It is based on solid science, even though part of the conclusion, as with all good science, is conjecture and surmise: that more research and scientific enquiry will reveal evidence to support or deny the original hypothesis. This is particularly important for Lovelock, as he continues in his nineties to confound those who wish to pigeonhole him as a greenie environmentalist, and, in a term that resonates with the onslaught that Carson experienced, as a tree hugger. For example, paradoxically for some, he has been an advocate of nuclear power. He is both excited and gloomy about his prediction that by the end of this century billions of people will die, because nature is not benign, and there might be just a few people remaining, living in the Arctic. As social philosopher John Gray says of Lovelock's work: 'the Earth system will respond [to the human impact] so as to restore some kind of balance, regardless of human plans. Finally dislodging the human animal from primacy in the

18 James Hutton, *Theory of the Earth; or an Investigation of the Laws Observable in the Composition, Dissolution, and Restoration of Land upon the Globe* (Sioux Falls, SD: NuVision Publications, 2007 [1788]): 75.

world.' In this sense, Gray believes, and Lovelock postulates, 'the Gaia theory can be seen as completing Darwin's work'.[19]

Lovelock, unlike Darwin, was born into a relatively poor family – his mother worked in a pickle factory and his father had been to prison for poaching – and he relied initially on the local public library in Brixton for his reading and later on the support of his employer to get his first degree. Just as Darwin was passionate about the fate of humanity and an enlightened social activist, so too Lovelock is a great supporter of universal healthcare free at the point delivery, as served by the UK's National Health Service. This seems to run contrary to his avowed belief that the extrapolation from the science means that humanity has little chance of continuing on Earth beyond this century, partly because of the damage it has brought upon itself. While atheistic commentators like Richard Dawkins and Christopher Hitchens may criticise Lovelock, because they see him as promoting a set of religious beliefs, and some on the left and in the green movement may lambast him for not being human-centric enough, and therefore apparently not concerned enough for common humanity, they are both to my mind misunderstanding Lovelock's work and positioning.[20]

The Earth is a self-balancing living entity within the cosmos, operating within the laws of science and subject to much further investigation. This does not make his theory god-like, indisputable or non-mysterious – or mysterious. I find it quite possible to accept his idea and also to believe that there is more to know. If I am exhibiting symptoms of schizophrenia, then I'm in good company – with Darwin, Lovelock, Galileo, Hawking

19 John Gray, 'Man for All Seasons', *New Statesman*, 22–28 March 2013: 34.
20 See, for instance, Colin Blakemore, 'Interview with James Lovelock', *The Observer*, 12 June 2011: 21.

and many others. Richard Dawkins's 1982 book *The Extended Phenotype* argued that Gaia theory seemed to imply some form of altruism attributable to the Earth's self-regulation; but this application of a moral attribute to natural systems is not my interpretation of Lovelock's science. Lovelock is simply (it's not simple at all, of course) talking about the extraordinary conditions that apparently have occurred for Earth, and on Earth. This is not a form of consciousness at all, as people like Dawkins are asserting, but it provides an apparent extension for our consciousness. It is more in the realms of Jung's collective consciousness, Bateson's ecology of mind and Capra's hidden connections.

James Lovelock's frequent walks with Nobel Laureate William Golding around the countryside near Bowerchalke in Dorset, England, where they both then lived, must have been a treat. What a subject they would make for a novel or a film script! Lovelock, the pacifist cosmologist and physicist, in company with Golding, the former Naval engineer and classics expert turned novelist. Lovelock's nonconformism is well suited to the use of metaphor – and helps the non-scientist to understand the science – so this friendship would have been mutually reinforcing. Golding had been trained as a scientist and an engineer, unlike most novelists. As his biographer John Carey says, all Golding's novels are concerned in some way or other with '[bringing] into collision, to some degree, two different ways of thinking about the world, pitting logic, reason and science on the one hand against religion and imagination on the other'. As Carey points out, any hopes that the Enlightenment would see the end of 'religion, with its hopes and terrors' and that religion 'would evaporate in the face of progress' is far from true.[21] Indeed, there is a strong line of thought which suggests that faith, trust and belief are part of what it means to be human: that they are part of our evolutionary DNA. To do good science is to be sceptical, to trust so far, and to believe that more is possible. But while respecting awe and a sense of the unknown we must not get bogged down by religiosity and organisational dogma.

And so to what we know, now. According to the IPCC's 5th Assessment Report in 2013, there has been a 40% rise in the concentration of atmospheric CO_2 between 1750 and 2011.[22] There is a 95% certainty that climate change has anthropomorphic origins and this is agreed by the vast majority of internationally acclaimed climate change scientists globally – 97% of climate change scientists to date. We have the highest levels of CO_2, methane and nitrous oxide in 800,000 years and the oceans have absorbed one-third of carbon emitted causing acidification. 'Global warming' is a misnomer – it should be called climate change, as it increasingly is by those who appreciate the complexities. We have 30 years to act or it will be too late. But, even so, the carbon in the air would take 1,000 years to be absorbed. We are already seeing extreme contrasts between wet and dry seasons in many parts of the world and these incidents will increase.

21 John Carey, *William Golding: The Man who Wrote* Lord of the Flies (London: Faber & Faber, 2009): 520.
22 One of my climate change science colleagues has pointed out that 'using percentages without the actual data is poor practice – but common in journalism circles' especially when trying to make points about the idea of climate change. So, even though I have been a journalist and am now a social scientist, I would refer the reader to the IPCC website in order that these figures are understood in context: www.ipcc.ch.

In 1972 the first World Conference on the Environment was held in Stockholm, and in 1987 *Our Common Future*, the Brundtland Report, was published, with its now standard and oft-repeated definition of sustainable development. In 1989 Margaret Thatcher, acting on the inspiration of the UK's ambassador to the UN, Crispin Tickell, gave a speech to the UN General Assembly on global warming in which she warned that climate change would change everything. At this time she didn't mention any links to economics and did not seem aware that her beloved economic neoliberalism would make matters worse not better.

The 1992 Rio Earth Summit produced various declarations and was the first world conference on sustainable development. It was followed by the 2002 Johannesburg Earth Summit which acknowledged the role that business played and could play in the future. The 2012 Rio+20 Earth Summit in Brazil similarly worked on a trisector basis and, similarly, produced numerous normative statements, most of which have been ignored.

The upward trend of the numbers continues: between 1950 and 2000 the population of the planet doubled from 3 to 6 billion, and between the start of the industrial revolution, in the mid eighteenth century, and 2013 there was a 140% increase in CO_2 emissions into the atmosphere.

Why refer to nuclear warfare when discussing climate change? Because in both cases we know the science; in both cases we have a disconnect between scientists, technologists and politicians; and in both cases we have the power to do something – but will we? Not unless we stand and stare and reflect.

At 5.30 am on 16th July 1945 the first atom bomb was detonated in the New Mexico desert. Less than a month later the US went on to drop an atomic bomb and a thermonuclear device on the Japanese cities of Hiroshima and Nagasaki. Robert Oppenheimer, the Director of the Manhattan Project which developed this technology of mass destruction, said that humans now not only had the capacity to destroy all life on Earth but also they knew that they had this capacity. Quoting from the Bhagavad Gita, he said: 'we have become Death, the destroyer of worlds'. 'The physicists have known sin.'[23] This was the end of innocence.

Rachel Carson was inspired by Beatrix Potter's multidisciplinary approach – both embodied the spirit of Renaissance women – and both challenged the hegemonic domination of men and of the status quo. Potter, a Lakelands woman but born in London, was inspired by the poet William Wordsworth who wrote of beauty and the inner eye, and against formal education, it being a form of enslavement (but I wonder if he also understood it as empowerment and a social mobiliser?). Both Beatrix Potter's and Rachel Carson's language and demeanour were inspired by the image of mother Earth as the wholeness and giver of life, the nurturer and procreator in distinction to the dominance, destruction and competition of masculinity. As women writing about science, their message is positive news for humanity, so long as an understanding of evolution is based on the feminisation of knowledge.

23 For more on the bombing of Hiroshima and Nagasaki and the development of weapons of mass destruction, see Malcolm McIntosh, *Japan Re-armed* (repr. edn; London: Bloomsbury, 2013 [1986]).

3

Co-existence, peace and feminisation

In this chapter I have used the term 'feminisation' to represent ideas of nurturing, caring, sharing and social cohesion. The feminisation of society and governance is one way of looking at the growth of the idea of social democracy – that potentially it produces societies where conflict is minimised, where the collective is balanced with the individual, and where competitive effort and human rights are upheld. In the ideal social democracy, men and women have equal rights, and children and the vulnerable are protected. In this model form of social democracy discussion, negotiation and the rule of law are everyday ways of being, and violence and aggression are minimised as ways of solving disputes. This takes away the advantage in dispute outcomes of the physically strong, the violent and the masculine. Advanced social democracies also have significant gun control and an absence of the death penalty as the ultimate state penalty.

Observations of advanced social democracies also show that, beyond the mechanics of discussion and negotiation, the enforcement of law and the management of democratic institutions, there is an evolution of more gentle ways of acting out. This advantages the quiet and allows the otherwise silent to be heard: 'the other' get a word in. It allows children and women to be heard, and diversity to be recognised against the roar of the loud and vexatious – and against the dominant and the masculine. It allows for women to have equal representation and it allows for space to be created to allow women, children and the quiet to be heard: it creates windows for listening. In this space it also allows for quiet, gentle men to speak who would otherwise have been crowded out by their aggressive, macho counterparts. In a similar way the evolution of civilised thinking meant that, during the Second World War, men in the UK were no longer shot or ostracised for refusing to fight as conscientious objectors to war.

The evolution of organised sport has had a similarly civilising effect, with tribal enmity and physical aggression released under strictly refereed rules. Imperfect though they are, the FIFA World Cup and the Olympic Games are wonderful manifestations of our evolution, adaptation and learning as less violently aggressive human beings. They allow global competition to take place at the highest level without blood being spilled and without war taking place.

Social democracy, the organisation of global sport, and the development of global human rights are all examples of the feminisation of society: of a rebalancing of feminine and masculine. This may be thought of as *re*-feminisation, given that there have been periods in the past when some societies were more balanced than today.

Today, rather than nurturing warlords and warriors, the development of management and life skills increasingly emphasises social capitalisation, negotiation and team building. This has led to the feminisation of men, producing more rounded, softer carers-for-others rather than out-and-out slayers.

To make the point *in extremis*, I want to quote Tsutomu Yamaguchi, who survived the atomic bombing of Hiroshima and 'escaped' to Nagasaki, only to be bombed again. He died in 2010 aged 93:

> The only people who should be allowed to govern countries [with nuclear weapons] are mothers, those who are still breastfeeding babies.

But in a world of feminised men, there would be no such dilemma.

French philosopher and semiotician Roland Barthes asked, 'Who will write the history of tears? In which societies, in which periods have we wept? Since when is it that men (and not women) no longer cry? Why was "sensibility", at a certain moment, transformed into "sentimentality"?'[1] A recent example of wonderful writing in this area comes from Colm Tóibín's *Testament of Mary*, as she, Jesus's mother, looks up at him (Jesus Christ, the heroic man) nailed to the cross:

> I gasped when I saw the cross ... It was when I caught his eye that things changed ... He was a boy I had given birth to and he was more defenceless now than he had been then ...
>
> In those days if I had even dreamed that I would see him bloody, and the crowd around filled with

---

1 Roland Barthes quoted in Susan Sontag, *Writing Itself: On Roland Barthes – A Reader* (London: Vintage, 1993): 427.

zeal that he should be bloodied more, I would have cried out that day and that cry that would be have come from that part of me that is the core of me. The rest of me is merely flesh and blood and bone.

For the nailing part, we stood back . . . I tried to see his face as he screamed in pain . . . I stood and looked around. There were other things going on – horses being shoed and fed, games being played, insults and jokes being hurled, and fires lit to cook food, with the smoke rising and blowing around the hill.[2]

In our here-and-now, over-rational and masculine world, there is little space for sentimentality, reflection or tears in decision-making forums and procedures. But, as social democracy advances and becomes normalised over the next few decades, we will see a greater emphasis on consideration of those things that make life more rounded.

The human pacification process

In *Humanity: A Moral History of the Twentieth Century,* Jonathan Glover, a moral philosopher, pointed out that although the first half of the century had been the bloodiest in human history the second half had shown that, having reached the brink of extermination, the world was as peaceful as it has ever been; that, in reality, it was becoming more peaceful, despite extreme random and localised violent events.[3] And, in *The*

2 Colm Tóibín, *The Testament of Mary* (London: Penguin, 2012): 73.
3 Jonathan Glover, *Humanity: A Moral History of the Twentieth Century* (New Haven, CT: Yale University Press, 2001).

THINKING THE TWENTY-FIRST CENTURY

Better Angels of our Nature, Steven Pinker, a behavioural psychologist, pointed out that we are becoming a more peaceful species, and that peacefulness is breaking out everywhere. He claims that as a species humans are coming to understand that cooperation is more beneficial to us all than tribal or national enmity.[4]

Fatalities inflicted by wars

Source: Steven Pinker, *The Better Angels of our Nature: A History of Violence and Humanity* (London: Penguin, 2012).

	Death toll	Equivalent death toll if event had happened mid 20th century
1. An Lushan Revolt, China, C8th	36,000,000	429,000,000
2. Mongol Conquests, Asia and Eastern Europe, C13th	40,000,000	278,000,000
3. Mid-East slave trade, C7th–9th	19,000,000	132,000,000
4. Fall of Ming Dynasty, China, C17th	25,000,000	112,000,000
5. Fall of Rome, Europe, C3rd–5th	8,000,000	105,000,000
6. Timur Lenk (Tamerlane), Central Asia, C14th–15th	17,000,000	100,000,000
7. Annihilation of Native Americans, C15th–19th	20,000,000	92,000,000
8. Atlantic slave trade, C15th–19th	18,000,000	83,000,000
9. Second World War, C20th	55,000,000	55,000,000
10. Taiping Rebellion, C19th	20,000,000	40,000,000

4 Steven Pinker, *The Better Angels of our Nature: A History of Violence and Humanity* (London: Penguin, 2012).

123

Other evidence of our increasing global peacefulness can be gleaned from the annual UN Development Report's Human Development Index, the recently launched Global Peace Index and other sources. Even the CIA's annual yearbook is testimony to peace breaking out. They all point to less inter-state warfare, yet continuing intrastate conflict; to an increasing number of countries that can be classified as democracies, albeit with some stretching of the definition; and to the dramatically increased use of social media for activities ranging from banking to personal relationships to education, all of which cross national boundaries with alacrity and have no respect for territoriality.

Despite the apparent sense of the coming apocalypse as a result of extreme climate change conditions, human progress has advanced in leaps and bounds since the end of the last world war in 1945.

Global connectivity, collaboration and regard for social and environmental nurturing are also dominant themes in business initiatives such as 'Conscious Capitalism', led by leading US academics like Darden's Ed Freeman and business people, and 'The B Team', led by Richard Branson, Jochen Zeitz and John Elkington. Similarly, more established corporate responsibility initiatives like the UN Global Compact, launched in 1999, propose that it is possible to marry public policy goals and private policy making and use the market to help deliver public goods. These initiatives in remodelling capitalism have in common a desire to lead the debate beyond the management technologies of transparency, accountability, reporting and good governance to a higher place where the culture of the company and leadership is of itself nurturing of social and environmental capital.

This could be a remodelling of capitalism and corporate interest (and therefore be seen as an attempt to save capitalism and business) based on partnership becoming collaboration, profit becoming a concomitant outcome rather than the be-all and end-all of business, and leaders becoming carers of social cohesion and environmental protection and nurturers of people – in other words, soft-skilled and feminised rather than hard-task and masculine. All of which leads to a discussion about 'the feminisation of management and leadership'.

The harmonised society: a balance between feminine and masculine

A feminine society, and feminised management, offer a softer, more caring and nurturing approach which takes into account emotional, social and environmental concerns, alongside economic issues. The feminine society has determined goals and is not without targets, but is clear in its determination to be nurturing in its approach. In other words, rethinking what is meant by 'the good society' means taking into account many of the characteristics of the feminine, which is not necessarily the same as a woman's way but would be highly correlative. What then are the implications for society and governance systems?

In *The Better Angels of our Nature*, Steven Pinker says, 'feminization is the process in which cultures have increasingly respected the interests and values of women'.[5] He means to talk about women, but it is also easy to talk about respecting the interests and the values that women represent. It is not just women that need representing, supporting and promoting but also a different way of doing things, a different way of making decisions, based on a different way of seeing the world.

5 Pinker, *The Better Angels of our Nature*: xxvi.

Discussions about 'women *and* power' or about 'women *in* power' are very important in moves towards a feminine society, but they are subsets of the larger task of humanising decision-making, of seeing decision-making through a feminine lens. This is not the same as a feminist society or an effeminate society although a feminine society could encompass both and would most certainly mean at least a balance of men and women at all levels of decision-making. The feminisation of society should, in the context of this line of thought, mean the humanisation of global governance, or global governance for human-scale living. Through harmonisation and a rebalance of feminine and masculine we could reach a higher level of consciousness.

Does such a thing as a feminine society exist? According to colleagues and my family, no it doesn't. I have been told repeatedly that 'there are only masculine societies at present'. If this is true – and I'm not so sure myself – what would a feminine society look like? What would be its characteristics?

In setting out on this journey there is a wealth of information on gender issues, data on women, power, education and health and ideas on development, growth and sustainability, but very little that spells out exactly what might be meant by the feminisation of society – or indeed the characteristics of the masculinity embedded in current models. There are signposts, some of which are referred to later, but the road leads all over the place. There is plenty of evidence that, to misquote Margaret Mead, 'never doubt what a small group of committed women can do to change the world', but I do not mean women, but women *and* men who have feminine attributes which I take to be more concerned with the many than the few.

By feminisation I mean characteristics that both men *and* women can display such as emotional intelligence, the knowledge that going it alone may not be the right path, and, that locking antlers only leads to a victor and a victim. It takes a community to raise a child, and so too it takes a sense of community to make decisions that are best for communities of people – young and old, men and women, rich and poor, well and not so well, mobile and less mobile, hirsute and bald. There is evidence that economic rationalism and an over-focus on the individual coupled with effective rather than affective communities online is leading to increased loneliness and suicide, particularly among men.

Men have been tracking down animals, riding out to stake a claim, being the first on the Poles and the Moon and up Everest, hitting the hardest ball, kicking the longest shot, and discovering 'the truth' since the beginning of human history. But what we have not kept such a close eye on is who is minding the children, who is gathering the crops and milking the cows, who is tending the wounded and holding the distressed. There are fewer heroes (or heroines) in this story of human history. Jared Diamond's 2013 book concerns the things we are losing by not remembering our dwindling isolated tribal communities; in it, he says, we lose a sense of our past at our peril.[6] So too we lose a sense of the part that nurturing men and women have contributed, at our peril.

This is particularly so at this time of immense change, disruption and transition for humankind. For some the major transition in the history of humanity currently under way is the cataclysmic effect of climate change; for others it's the depletion of natural resources; or the collapse of the international banking and finance system; or population and demographics; or the growing instability caused by nuclear weapons acquisition.

6 Diamond, *The World until Yesterday*.

For others, liberation and positive change are to be found in the growth of social media and the porosity of nation-state boundaries, which have helped foment discussion in China, helped organise the Arab Spring, and gave the Occupy movement life and made its sentiments global. So this transition point is also a moment to take stock of humanity's success and to understand our diversity *and* our homogeneity, our creativity and problem-solving abilities and our enterprising nature – and the feminine–masculine balance of societies around the world. Now that we are rapidly moving towards global citizenship, actual or virtual, it is also time to think about the feminisation of global rule-making and global governance.

In order to take care of the Earth – and ourselves – we need to move beyond the current model of development, which is based on growth, and move to a more caring, sharing, nurturing, reflective mode of being. We no longer need the emphasis to be on having and doing, but return to a balance of having, doing and *being*. Being. Here, now.

As anyone knows who has gently rocked a baby to sleep through the wee small hours of the dark night when all others are tucked up and soundly floating through their dreams, it takes time, infinite patience and, most of all, love. The greatest gift to a child is unconditional love, a nurturing family and a supportive community.

As I have mentioned previously, one of the pre-eminent founders of modern environmentalism, eighteenth-century geologist James Hutton, who also founded the Royal Geological Society and was ironically best friend and literary executor of 'the father of modern economics' Adam Smith, said, 'the meaning of life is life itself'.[7] In order to love life, we have to

7 Hutton, *The Theory of the Earth*. This can be downloaded for free from www.gutenberg.org/ebooks/12861.

love the planet, for it is the planet that bears us, that gives us life and takes us away, that confounds us, that gives us joy, that gives succour to our desire for sea and land, that lays bare the ground that our animals may bring forth calves, that opens itself that the trees may bear fruit. If this sounds biblical so be it, but it's also scientific. To love the Earth is to love our common home: planet Earth.

Our current model of capitalism is still, even in this century of growing planetary awareness, based on a model of expansion and limitless resource extraction. Physicist Fritjof Capra's 1982 book *The Turning Point* drew on the idea of the balance of yin and yang in all things to make the point that the world is currently unbalanced. It is too yang: too masculine, right-brained, aggressive, individualistic and conquering. This has led to the Earth being plundered not respected. We have forgotten (or did we ever know?) that we are not above nature, but part of it. The yin has become inferior and we are out of balance. We need to balance the whole and reintroduce awe, wonder and respect in our relationship with that which sustains us.[8] Yin has been regarded as a lower-order function.

Yin and yang are not a question of either–or but a respect for balance or a holistic view of all issues. Too much yang is implicit in 'scientific/rational' research and management theory and has led to too little light being cast on subjects such as trust, love and spirituality in business and management. Yin and yang combined offer not only a holistic or systems view, but also a dynamic view of interactions and synergies. It is important when recognising the yin, or feminine side of life, to understand that discounting either–or means that both yin and yang are equal components, but not opposites, of the whole. In

8 Capra, *The Turning Point.*

other words, both carry equal weight: to be one or the other is to be imbalanced.

So, being yin is not to be inferior or passive. Society needs both yin and yang, femininity and masculinity. Yin characteristics are feminine, collaborative, contractive, responsive, cooperative, emotional, creative, empathetic, intuitive and synthesising – and allow for fields of energy and flow. Yang characteristics are masculine, demanding, aggressive, competitive, objective, assertive, rational and analytic – and goal-directed. In traditional Chinese thinking, which pervades all Chinese and most of Asian philosophy, the night and the Moon are yin, and the day and the light are yang. The argument is that we have too much of the latter and not enough of the former, and that the good society needs a balance of all these characteristics. Further, it is suggested that the model of economics that is rampant (joke intended) worldwide, especially in neoliberalism, is very yang with little respect for yin. Indeed, to be intuitive, cooperative and non-aggressive is often presented at irrational and emotional – which are apparently very poor ways of making decisions!

Taking the men and the masculinity away

If it's not clear already, we are discussing three aspects of a similar idea, which are often confused and normally conflated, but which are not the same thing: women *and* power, women *in* power, and the feminisation of society. Both men and women can have feminine attributes, by which I most profoundly do not mean femininity, cross-dressing or any such caricature. I have begun to tackle what is meant by the feminisation of society. But let's start by briefly discussing women *and* power and women *in* power.

There is a long history of women and power that tends to show that women who have power in national, tribal or organisational settings exercise it in a very similar way to men. Very rarely can it be shown that when women have power have they made decisions that have led to more feminine societies. This is true of Elizabeth I's reign in England from 1558–1603, Golda Meir's Israeli premiership from 1969–1974, Madame Mao's substantial influence in China from 1966–1976, and Julia Gillard's premiership in Australia beginning in 2010. If anything, these women in power exemplify the need for the feminisation of management and governance as their periods in office underpinned masculine institutional and organisational structures rather than leading to reform, even if they highlight the role of women in power.[9]

The same is of course true of Prime Minister Margaret Thatcher's time in office in the UK. She had fewer women in her cabinet than in previous cabinets and she implemented policies that were family-, children- and women-unfriendly. It is generally recognised that her style was aggressive and combative and built not on consensus but on divisiveness. Indeed, she is famously remembered for having said that consensus

---

9 See, for example, Katherine Hepworth, 'Gillard's misogyny speech looks even better than it reads', *The Conversation* (Australia), 14 October 2012, and John Pilger, 'Julia Gillard is no feminist hero', *The Guardian*, 15 October 2012; www.theguardian.com/commentisfree/2012/oct/15/julia-gillard-no-feminist-hero, accessed 14 December 2014.

'is something in which no one believes and to which no one objects'.[10]

By comparison, Britain's greatest peacetime prime minister Clement Attlee was a quiet consensus builder, not a masculine rabble-rouser, who delivered one of the world's greatest gifts: the first free-at-the-point-of-delivery-for-all national health scheme, still the envy of the world. Attlee was the UK Labour Party leader for 20 years, British PM from 1945–1951, and served as Deputy PM with Winston Churchill in the WWII coalition government.

What matters is not simply having women in power, nor just the recognition of diversity, but what happens when there is diversity in power. At the moment, in most countries, but not all, women who have power by virtue of being *in* power are more likely to be more masculine than men because they have had to struggle harder in a man's world to reach the top. So, just having women in power is no guarantee of the feminisation of decision-making. Even so, let us be careful and make it clear that this is not to denigrate the idea of getting more women into power as this is an obvious first step, but, if these women are as masculine as the men who currently rule the roost the world over, we will make little progress in civilising and humanising our institutional and organisational structures and our rapacious model of capitalism.

There is of course an enormous imbalance in gender across almost all national and corporate institutions worldwide,

---

10 'To me, consensus seems to be the process of abandoning all beliefs, principles, values and policies. So it is something in which no one believes and to which no one objects – the process of avoiding the very issues that have to be solved, merely because you cannot get agreement on the way ahead' (Margaret Thatcher, speech at Monash University, 1981 [Sir Robert Menzies Lecture]).

despite the fact that all the evidence is that gender-balanced parliaments and corporate boards make better short-, medium- and long-term decisions than gender-skewed cabinets and boards. In some countries this is because women are simply not valued as equal human beings and do not have the same rights as men; some other countries have apartheid constitutional and legal apparatus in place to keep women out of power. In many countries the research shows that 'it's a man's world' and men actively keep women out of power because they feel threatened by them and the issues that they might raise and the way they make decisions. On the same basis, soft, gentle men are not valued.

What would happen if the UK parliament had family-friendly hours? Just look at how Barack Obama's second term as President of the USA was secured by more women voting for him than men because Obama had family- and women-friendly items on his agenda.[11] Just think of the real revolution on the streets of the Middle East and elsewhere if women were given equal access to education, driving licences, childcare facilities, and the seats of power!

Should the world be adopting the Norwegians' 2003 mandate for there to be at least 40% female representation on all corporate boards, or the Finnish example of requiring all companies to publicly explain why they do not have women on their boards? These two countries escaped the 2008 global financial crisis; every year they hit the top of the productivity and innovation rankings and score in the top five for educational

11 See Suzanne Goldenberg, 'Obama scored big with single women', *Guardian Weekly*, 16 November 2012: 4; Nicole Hemmer, 'It's the women wot won it: Democrat victory was not fluke', *The Conversation* (Australia), 8 November 2012; and Peter Kellner, 'Thank Fox for that', *Prospect* (UK), December 2012.

attainment. According to the UN HDI,[12] they come in the top ten for human development, and have booming economies based on a complex mix of economic activities. In other words, there appears to be a correlation between closing the gender gap and economic success, or to be even more specific, given the two examples of Norway and Finland and a real balance of men and women in power, the feminine and egalitarian society works on all levels. Egalitarian societies have numerous benefits, not least prosperity.

In the US, by comparison, women say that they have actively looked for board positions whereas men tend to have been appointed by their networks because 'men appoint men who think and act like them' and, yet, women on US boards have greater operational experience than men and are therefore better qualified to run the company than their male counterparts.[13]

In Australia, according to one survey, women are the most empowered in the world on a range of issues: education, childcare, equal pay and anti-discrimination, but their pay is still significantly lower than men's. On the basis of these indicators Australia ranks 25th out of 134 and has slipped from 15th in 2006. Iceland heads the list, followed by most Scandinavian countries along with Ireland, New Zealand, The Philippines, Nicaragua and Switzerland.[14] There are some surprises in researching this issue!

---

12 United Nations Development Programme Human Development Index: hdr.undp.org/en/statistics.

13 See, for example, Chris Lee, 'The Feminisation of Management', *Training* 31.11 (1994): 25-31.

14 Strategy&, 'The Third Billion: As growing numbers of women enter the economic mainstream, they will have a profound effect on global business', Strategy&, 2012; www.strategyand.pwc.com/global/home/what-we-think/third_billion, accessed 1 December

Even if women are in power, it may not mean that decision-making and management becomes more caring, sharing and nurturing. Many surveys show that it is only when something like 30% of senior decision-makers are women in any one organisation, be it national or corporate, that the style, tone and content of decision-making changes significantly.

So, can we find examples of feminine societies and what might they look like? How might this have a direct impact on feminising global governance and thereby changing the way global issues are dealt with?

Anthropologist Geert Hofstede started looking at a range of national cultural difference indicators in 1980, and his son, Gert, has continued the work. Their five cultural differentiators are: power distance, individualism, masculinity/femininity, uncertainty avoidance, and long-term orientation. Masculinity in society is described as 'competition, achievement and success, with success being defined by the winner or best in field – a value system that starts in school and continues throughout organisational behavior'. Femininity in society is described as follows: 'the dominant values in society are caring for others and quality of life'. According to Hofstede's analysis, 'a feminine society is one where quality of life is the sign of success and standing out from the crowd is not admirable. The fundamental issue here is what motivates people, wanting to be the best (masculine) or liking what you do (feminine)'.[15]

On this basis, Australia is a masculine society with a highly individualistic culture; the UK is similarly masculine and highly individualistic but less able to handle uncertainty; and Japan

---

2014; and Clay Lucas, 'Women most empowered in world but men still rule the roost on pay', *Sydney Morning Herald*, 17 October 2012; bit.ly/1zfxjkW, accessed 14 December 2014.

15 geert-hofstede.com/dimensions.html.

is extremely masculine and low on individualism. What Hofstede's analysis misses is the fact that competition in Japan is shown not between individuals but between groups, in corporate or team form. This is, to some extent, the antithesis of the Australian and US definition of masculinity, where competition tends to be a sign of individualism.

In terms of what is meant in this essay by the feminisation of society, Hofstede's very interesting and useful work also does not recognise other issues in this redefinition of the good society. A balance of yin and yang, or femininity and masculinity, would put more emphasis on harmony and less emphasis on growth, expansion, individualism, triumph, pioneering, battle and domination. A balance of yin and yang necessarily produces harmony, so that the third attribute of the good society is a natural result of the balance between the two essential characteristics found in yin and yang. This three-point model – yin, yang and harmony – is often noted in Chinese and Japanese literature and storytelling.

For those who may want to dismiss this new model as unrealistic, impractical, and not allied to the history of humanity, or anti-men (yes, men with low emotional intelligence will feel threatened in some cultures – indeed, they may not have a clue what the feminisation of society is all about!), this triangular way of seeing society is as old as the hills in one sense because some of its aspects can be seen in pre-industrial societies, by which I mean pre-industrial capitalism, pre-Protestant work-ethic societies. And most of its characteristics can be glimpsed in countries around the world, even if most societies are at present predominantly masculine.

We might look at particular sectors of business or society rather than focusing on particular countries, as this categorisation – the nation-state – is maybe too rigid a way of seeing the world in the twenty-first century. As much of the literature on the 2008/9 financial credit crash reveals, there are very few women in the stories. Reading Robert Peston's *How Do We Fix This Mess?* or Andrew Ross Sorkin's *Too Big to Fail* or John Lanchester's *Why Everyone Owes Everyone and No One Can Pay* is to understand a very male and masculine world full of risk, aggression and competition. As Gillian Tett from the *Financial Times* says, 'in two decades of reporting on central bank activity I have met very few senior women'.[16] (The appointment in 2012 and 2013 of Christine Lagarde to run the IMF and Janet Yellen to run the US Federal Reserve is a step in the right direction but, without momentum and the numbers, it is tokenistic.)

One book on the crisis that points out this male bias is Michael Lewis's *The Big Short*. Lewis is reported to have recommended the one single action he would take to stop the crisis repeating: 'I would take steps to have 50% of women in risk positions in banks.'[17] It is well known that women do

16 Gillian Tett, 'Central Banking: Still a Man's World', *FT.com/magazine*, 10–11 August 2013; Robert Peston, *How Do We Fix This Mess? The Economic Price of Having it All, and the Route to Lasting Prosperity* (London: Hodder & Stoughton, 2012); Andrew Ross Sorkin, *Too Big to Fail: Inside the Battle to Save Wall Street* (London: Viking, 2009); John Lanchester, *Whoops! Why Everyone Owes Everyone and No One Can Pay* (London: Allen Lane, 2010); John Lanchester, 'How to speak money – and why you need to learn', *The Telegraph*, 9 August 2014; www.telegraph.co.uk/culture/books/11022772/How-to-speak-money-and-why-you-need-to-learn, accessed 1 December 2014.

17 Tim Adams, 'Testosterone and high finance do not mix: So bring on the women', *The Observer*, 19 June 2011; www.theguardian.com/world/2011/jun/19/neuroeconomics-women-city-financial-crash, accessed 14 December 2014; see also Lewis, *The Big Short*.

not take the risks that men take in most aspects of life, be it household finance, car insurance or mortgaging. Single women beat married women who beat men when it comes to investing household finances significantly as a household study in the US showed in 2001.[18]

Maleness in the dealing room is important, and, as in the military the language of masculinity and aggression is paramount. One former trader, now a research fellow in neuroscience and finance at Cambridge University, John Coates, said of his trading days: 'When I was making a lot of money I felt unbelievably powerful. You carry yourself like a strutting rooster, and you can't help it. Michael Lewis talked about "Big Swinging Dicks", Tom Wolfe talked about "Masters of the Universe" – they were right.'[19] Coates's colleague, endocrinology professor Joe Herbert, says the neurological differences between men and women are significant: 'Women, in very general terms, are less competitive, and less concerned with the status of being successful. If you want to make women more present, you have to remember two things: the world they are coming into is a man-made world. The financial world. So, either they become surrogate men . . . or you change the world.'[20]

In the USA and the UK the percentage of women serving as executive directors in FTSE 100 companies is less than 6%, and in Australia and Japan the figure is even lower. And yet the evidence from countries like Norway, which has a mandatory 40% quota for women on corporate boardrooms, appears to show improved results and certainly no poorer performance

---

18 Brad M. Barber and Terrance Odean, 'Boys Will Be Boys: Gender, Overconfidence, and Common Stock Investment', *Quarterly Journal of Economics* 116.1 (2001): 261-92.
19 Adams, 'Testosterone and high finance do not mix': 13.
20 Adams, 'Testosterone and high finance do not mix': 15.

with the upside that 50% of the population are being empowered and entitled to enter this male world.

To cut to the chase, the feminine, or good, society has some of the following characteristics. It is high on care and compassion, but not at the expense of enterprise and entrepreneurship. It takes time to reflect and ponder, providing physical spaces and political understanding for contemplation, conversation and well-informed, reasoned debate. Sitting around chatting as well as spending time meditating are regarded as good things, and not to be banished by the inane white noise of much social media and advertising or aggressive male bantering and point scoring. Above all, it recognises that collaboration and cooperation are absolute necessities, because ... Just as it takes a village to raise a child, it takes a community to build social cohesion and look after the sick, the oppressed, the disabled and the vulnerable. As Mahatma Gandhi said: 'A nation's greatness is measured by how it treats its weakest members.'

Humans are an enterprising, creative, designing, problem-solving species whose biogenetic emphasis has been on the balance of guarding the cave entrance *and* bringing food in to feed the cave's inhabitants. As economist Amartya Sen rightly says – in a slightly less straightforward manner – conversation, sharing and caring, fucking and procreation, exchange and being enterprising are essential parts of what it means to be human. But how can we make enterprise a spur to ingenuity serving all humanity and not simply a conduit for individual greed? This requires reworking our current capitalist model to make it more balanced and harmonious. We might want to call it yin–yang capitalism.

Another aspect of redefining the good society, via feminisation and a rebalance between yin and yang, includes conflict resolution and low crime – particularly against children and women. In many respects, it differs markedly from Plato's 'good society', although the emphasis on philosophy, representation and the necessity of a belief in the idea of the state or society is maintained. It is interesting to note that even Plato's good society is antithetical to Margaret Thatcher's view of every person as selfish, individualistic, rational market actors. According to the Thatcher line of thought, society is something that occurs through the actions of selfish individualism. She drew on Friedrich Hayek, who in turn claimed to draw on Adam Smith, which many would regard as a misreading of the morality of the political philosopher's work.[21]

This exploration of the feminisation of society is at an early stage, but some of the characteristics of this particular model of the good society can be found around the world – with plenty of paradox. For example, South Americans tend to have low-carbon, Earth-centric economies where people have low levels of neurosis and high levels of happiness, but rather masculine cultures and high levels of inequality and crime; the Japanese have created over hundreds of years a very peaceful, and extremely low-crime, society with high levels of social cohesiveness, politeness, civility and culture but an extreme gender gap and a reputation for gross insensitivity towards non-Japanese people; and Scandinavian countries have managed to develop significant social cohesion, low crime rates, and the world's best gender equality as well as national health services, but with relatively large carbon footprints and a reliance on the depletion of natural resources.

So, nowhere is perfect. But we can see that the feminisation of society, or the good society, through understanding the relationship between harmony and yin and yang, is very possible.

21 Friedrich Hayek's most influential work was *The Road to Serfdom* (1944).

We need to challenge the pioneering growth model of domination of each other and our natural habitat. The feminisation of society is an idea in development. Keep up the enterprise, but restore the balance. Be contemplative *and* active. Dream, care, strive and love. How do we build these fundamentals into our economic model?

Earlier I referred to a few new business initiatives which embrace the virtues of business and leadership models that nurture our feminine aspects of caring, sharing, nurturing and collaboration. For their obvious worth, what these initiatives lack is a coherent model of political economy that marries the often differing priorities of civil, public and private society and combines a philosophy of life based on an understanding of the co-ownership of planetary resources and our shared social future. I further argue that the new political economy should be based on feminine characteristics. The task is to marry the feminisation of governance to remodelling capitalism that nurtures social and environmental capital.

4

Re-organising and the political economy

This book began by referring to the 2012 UN High Level Report *Resilient People, Resilient Planet* which called for a new international political economy that would include objectives such as sustainable development and welfare issues:

> For too long, economists, social scientists and social activists and environmental scientists have talked past each other – almost speaking different languages, or at least different dialects. The time has come to unify the disciplines, to develop a common language for sustainable development that transcends the warring camps; in other words, to bring the sustainable development paradigm into mainstream economics ... That is why the Panel argues that the international community needs

what some have called 'a new political economy'
for sustainable development.[1]

One of the greatest challenges we face in an interdependent, neurally networked twenty-first century was summed up by a prescient Aristotle several thousand years ago, before we were technically wired: 'In a democracy if you have a small number of rich people, and a large number of poor people, the poor people will try to seize the rich people's assets. The answer is either reducing democracy or reducing poverty.'[2] Or, as the Danes say, 'If someone comes at you with a knife, it's probably because the other hand is holding a fork.'

Aristotle's democracy was not unlike the world today. Only some could vote, and only some people had power and the bias was very much in favour of rich men. Today there are those who would reduce or diminish democracy for their own ends, and today what we mean by democracy is up for discussion in a world where mass connectivity and participation are matched by total surveillance, instant gratification and systems instability. A corporate launches a new superficial singing star on the world and a male-led, violence-based wartribe post a beheading online. Meanwhile, the singing star is banned among religious fundamentalist groups because she sings of girl power and sex and the terrorist (for this is pure terror) group win more through their expert use of social media and virtual reality than on the territorial battlefield of men, muscle and arms. And everyone is using the same technology to disseminate information: terrorists, governments, civil society and business.

1 United Nations Secretary-General's High-Level Panel on Global Sustainability, *Resilient People, Resilient Planet*: Overview, 5.
2 Aristotle, *Politics*.

The evolution and adaptation of capitalism

Capitalism, like justice, education and freedom, is an idea that can't and won't go away. It was a term unheard of until the publication of Karl Marx's *Das Kapital* in 1867 and was never used by the man often cited as 'the modern founder of capitalism', Adam Smith. As Marx, and Smith, were both moral philosophers as much as economists, capitalism is a term associated with the study of political economics rather than what is sometimes referred to as the 'science' of economics.

How many times have I been at academic symposia, street demonstrations and in classrooms and been told that 'capitalism is in crisis' or that 'capitalism is the devil's work' or 'capitalism is incompatible with equality'. And, obversely, there is often a reactionary attack against 'this attack on capitalism'. Most of the discussions are in reality discussions of political economy and not lambastings of the idea of capitalism. Also, many of the current discussions in the twenty-first century about capitalism are discussions about STCs (supraterritorial corporations) and/or banking. The liberalisations of the 1980s, driven by Prime Minister Margaret Thatcher in the UK and President Ronald Reagan in the USA with the intellectual support of the Chicago School of Economics, allowed banks to create money by creating credit. In the creation of credit the banks countered their avowed monetarist public policies which tried to control money supply. As Nobel Prize-winning economist Joseph Stiglitz says:

> The problem is not an excess of savings but a
> financial system that is more fixated on speculation
> than on fulfilling its societal role of intermediation
> between those with excess funds and those who

need more money, in which scarce savings are allocated to the investments of highest social returns.[3]

Research at Cambridge University on the relationship
between people, decision-making and money shows a significant lack of understanding of the digital–analogue interface.
As Joe Herbert, an endocrinologist, points out, banks 'know all
about computers and systems and markets but they know next
to nothing about the human machine sitting in front of screens
making decisions'.[4] Putting to one side the possible contradic-
tion of humans being machines, what 'the science of economics' lacks is the back-story – the yarn. We are soft in the body
and in the head, mostly.

It is the current model of capitalism that is in need of rapid
change and not the idea itself. To study Adam Smith, Karl
Marx or Thomas Piketty, or indeed Tony Judt or Colin Crouch,
is to read about the moral, social and political economy issues
involved in interpreting, enacting and implementing the idea
of capitalism. I dispute that capitalism is per se a bad idea, or
has a tendency to bad. Capitalism simply means investment
of some sort in an idea for a return of some sort with the risk
taker being allowed to retain some of the rewards. This is why
the ideas behind capitalism, such as risk, investment, returns,
property rights, the rule of contract, and management, come
back for discussion on a regular basis. It is not capitalism that
is normally being discussed, but management and governance
issues.

It is the current organs, institutions and ways and means of
capitalism that are to blame for the apparent current crisis.

3 Joseph Stiglitz, 'Mired in Malaise: Stiglitz on Martin Wolf', *Financial Times*, 30–31 August 2014: 8.
4 Adams, 'Testosterone and high finance do not mix'.

It is not the idea of capitalism that is wrong, but the current interpretation.

If the 'capital' is only financial and is blind to social and environmental investment, and if the returns are only measured in monetary terms, then it will inevitably fail to satisfy the wider and more complex societal inclinations for the good society.

The new capitalism is neither left nor right, nor classical, neoliberal nor Marxist. The new capitalism is based on connectivity, accountability, transparency, networks, values, relationships, enablement, entrepreneurship and rethinking the meaning of capital: it can be financial, environmental, cultural, manufactured or social. It mirrors the new cosmological and neuroscience understanding of field theory: the space between things is more important that the things themselves. These spaces are energies. We have objectified too much. And we have created institutional arrangements that support complex financial systems that are out of control and have been set to reward those inside more than society as whole.

Freedom, Chile and neoliberal violence

The previous chapters have laid down the premises for this chapter on organising principles. Some of our institutions come naturally – the family, the village and myths, for instance – while many others have developed over the millennia due the state of our knowledge and environmental conditions – tribes, nation-states, corporations and, in the last few decades, virtual networks. I have argued that this century means coming to terms with realising one shared space, and I have called this globality; that there is a necessity to rebalance what we think we know and can do with a sense of wonder, and I have called this rebalancing science and awe; that sharing one space and taking time to acknowledge the limits of knowing, being and doing require a new way of managing, and I have called this the feminisation of governance; and, that many of our institutional arrangements and organisations are not suitable and this chapter is therefore called *re*-organising.

In the Age of Globality, and as we look towards the New Space Age, the biggest impediments to reasonable global governance are nationalism, tribalism and masculinity. Increasingly, the units of currency and power are cities and corporations and the issue is how to make them more efficient, more responsive and more accountable. And the issues are the same in both cases, but at present time both are subsumed within nation-states and their hold on, literally, inter*national* governance regimes.

How can we, us individuals, be both located and grounded in *affective* communities and yet virtually connected and concerned in *effective* global communities? How can we be both local and global citizens, and how can government and corporations be responsible to both local and global citizenships? We are still developing the ideas that Thomas Paine wrote of in *The Age of Reason* in 1794:

> Independence is my happiness, and I view things
> as they are, without regard to place or person; my
> country is the world, and my religion is to do good.

And in *The Rights of Man* of 1791 Paine echoed his father's Quakerism:

> I do not believe in the creed professed by the Jew-
> ish Church, by the Roman church, by the Greek
> church, by the Turkish church, by the Protestant

church, nor by any church that I know of. My own
mind is my own church . . . All national institutions
of churches, whether Jewish, Christian or Turkish,
appear to me no other than human inventions, set
up to terrify and enslave mankind, and monopolize
power and profit.[5]

The conditions become easier for the realisation of Paine's
global citizenship, or cosmopolitanism, through the realisation
of globality and Earth awareness. I have spent a lifetime flying
round the Earth, and, due to the wonders of crossing the date-
line when flying from Sydney to Santiago in Chile (a fifteen-
hour flight), you arrive at the same time as you take off. What
has actually happened is that you take off and hang suspended
in the air as the Earth passes beneath you. You travel nowhere
but the world moves on, the engines flailing desperately to keep
up in case you would fall backwards to the Earth, and yet,
because we want to feel we are making progress, day to day, we
believe we are going somewhere. If we stayed up long enough,
Sydney would pass beneath us and we could land imagining
that we had flown round the world when in reality time and
the Earth had flown by. This is relativism.

There are lots of dogs on the streets of Santiago, and most
of them look healthy and well fed, and all of them are non-
threatening and friendly. Some cities have dogs, but not like
this, beloved by all and friends to the citizens. How very coun-
terintuitive to discover that they are all looked after by the city
council and they have all been vaccinated and sterilised, and
they're all name-tagged. They are also fed by the citizens, who
love them. The people of Santiago, recognising that a dog is
man's best friend but that the city must be rid of them, voted

5 Thomas Paine, *The Theological Works of Thomas Paine* (London:
R. Carlile, 1824): 31.

for this humane end to the dog population. I'm told though that some people are breeding them to maintain a steady supply so there will always be healthy, happy dogs on Santiago's streets.

As I flew across the Pacific from my then home in Brisbane, Australia, to Santiago in Chile I watched Meryl Streep play Margaret Thatcher in *The Iron Lady*, the 2011 film, as she disintegrated into dementia and forgetfulness. It's a sad film and I watched in admiration of the actress Streep not the politician Thatcher; but by the end I was touched by Streep's portrayal of the end of life, of loneliness and forgetfulness, of the demise of power, status and position. In the end we are all but dust to dust, ashes to ashes, stardust to the cosmos. How many former senior politicians and business people have I known who have become wise, compassionate and humanitarian in their retirement. They all say that while in the thick of it they had no time to think. So, one recommendation for power is to find time to meditate, or, like Churchill find time to paint watercolours or build a brick wall with your hands. During one summer break Václav Havel wrote a book on power, *Summer Meditations*, as I have noted previously. How rare for these leaders to be reflective practitioners. To find quiet to wonder, and not be lost.

In Chilean Patricio Guzmán's 2010 film *Nostalgia de la luz* (*Nostalgia for the Light*) three searches converge. In the driest place on Earth – the Atacama Desert in Chile – cosmologists look into the clear night sky in search of the beginnings of the Big Bang; in the desert archaeologists look for the remains of pre-Colombian people; and in the same desert mothers look for the remains of their loved ones, the *desaparecidos* – political prisoners, whose bodies were scattered in this place by the Pinochet regime in the 1970s.

Pinochet's military overthrow of the democratically elected Marxist government in 1973 was aided by the US and the CIA and some large US multinational companies, and endorsed by Prime Minister Margaret Thatcher in the UK. She also supported General Pinochet when he came to Britain as an old man and was wanted for crimes against humanity. They were all disciples of Friedrich Hayek whose political economics now dominates global financial systems.

For Chileans, 9/11 doesn't mean the destruction of the twin towers in New York, bad though that was. For Chileans 9/11 is 9/11/73 and is much worse. Some 30,000 people who opposed Pinochet's rule and his economics are still unaccounted for, many lost in the desert where they were housed in an old mining village, hundreds of kilometres from any other town.

Nostalgia de la luz is a film about the past which makes a connection between two important elements of the past: our cosmological origins as stardust left over from the Big Bang, and our Earthly and presently human past as inheritors of generations of history, evolution, adaptation and learning. As one of the cosmologists in Guzmán's film says:

> In as much as we are human beings, we are the inheritors of generations upon generations going back to prehistory, and the matter of our bodies is the matter of the stars. We belong to the Milky Way – that's our home, not just the Earth.

And, as another cosmologist in the film explains about time: 'between when I say "this is me" and when I touch my face there is a lapse in time'. In this time the Big Bang took place and whole world we know and don't know took shape and form, and on and on.

Time may be a curved ball but it moves on relentlessly. Or it stands still and a moment is crystallised – like that time you first tasted *umami*, or made love, or that memory of a perfect day you have that is now distant but so clear you can describe every detail. Or when the skylark sings in the clear blue sky above my head.

In 1973 the then US Secretary of State Kissinger said: 'I don't see why we need to stand by and watch a country go communist due to the irresponsibility of its own people.'[6] The CIA, funded by ITT under the direction of President Richard Nixon, who later resigned in the face of impeachment for deceit and lying on a number of fronts, and Secretary of State Henry Kissinger began the process of destabilising the elected communist government of Chile led by a medical doctor and political activist Salvador Allende.

On Chile's 9/11 in 1973, Chilean armed forces supported by the US overthrew the elected government in Santiago, and Allende was killed. General August Pinochet assumed control of Chile and all democratic institutions were closed down. Pinochet adopted Friedrich Hayek as his political and economic guru. Anyone with any opposing voice was arrested and some 30,000 people 'disappeared'. Pinochet ruled ruthlessly for eighteen years. Even though the world knew of his actions, and even after being indicted for human rights abuses, he continued to receive support from Nixon, Kissinger and Margaret Thatcher because he was of the same economic ideological bent and they all shared a hatred of the idea of labour collectivism.

In a similar vein, Thatcher described Nelson Mandela as a 'grubby little terrorist' and said 'the ANC is a typical terrorist organisation . . . Anyone who thinks it is going to run the government in South Africa is living in cloud-cuckoo land.' Such

6 Pilar Aguilera and Ricardo Fredes (eds.), *Chile: The Other September 11. An Anthology of Reflections on the 1973 Coup* (Minneapolis, MN/Melbourne, VIC: Ocean Press, 2006): 12.

is what former Czech President Václav Havel calls 'the particularisms of the time' and 'the swirl of bad politics' of the average politician.

In the case of Chile's Allende, post-1973 Pinochet had all those who opposed him disposed of, and any cultural item that referred to the previous regime was destroyed, including the globally renowned poet Pablo Neruda's library and art collection. This was economic theory as fascism and totalitarianism. By contrast, Nelson Mandela became President of South Africa partly because the business community there recognised that the time had come to end more than seventy years of oppression and human rights abuses in order that South Africa could become part of the international trade system. In November 2010, Mandela magnanimously took tea with Thatcher at 10 Downing Street, she having previously refused to meet him.

The business of capitalism: slavery, wool and empire

In 1788 the British government, at the height of its imperial majesty, when it 'ruled' 33% of the world's peoples and 25% of the landmass, had to ask the (British) East India Company for permission to establish a penal settlement in Australia: the company had previously been granted the right to sail and trade in that area through an Act of Parliament.[7] In the sixteenth century, Elizabeth I had granted 218 merchants a monopoly of trade east of the Cape of Good Hope. These were effectively

7 Pembroke, *Arthur Phillip*.

state-controlled mercantile enterprises with a remit, and the agency, to expand British influence worldwide.

This model of mercantilism and national expansion is recorded by Major Watkin Tench, whom we encountered earlier:

> The *Mary Anne* transport arrived from England . . . she brought out convicts, by contract, at a specific sum for each person. But to demonstrate the effect of humanity and justice, of 144 female convicts embarked on board only three had died . . . and the rest landed in perfect health, all loud in praise of their conductor . . . name Munro . . . The advocates of humanity are not yet become too numerous: but those who practise its divine precepts, however humble or unnoticed be their station, ought not to sink into obscurity, unrecorded and unpraised, with the vile monsters who deride misery and fatten calamity.[8]

Four hundred years later the role of state-owned, or -controlled, enterprises is not dissimilar in advancing the influence of nation-states. In 2013, of the largest 100 companies 19 were state-owned enterprises – the majority Chinese, Russian or Brazilian. Nation-state expansion has always been initially carried out by traders and business interested in capturing raw materials, cheap labour and markets.

In 2014, the Anglo-Dutch food and cleaning conglomerate Unilever operates in 156 markets worldwide and its direct competitor, the US's Procter & Gamble, has some 4 billion regular customers worldwide. Just as in earlier centuries, in the twenty-first century it is corporations that often have the longest arms – now including information, data processing and

8 Tench, *1788*: 205.

telecommunications companies. But today the extent of corporate interests are under extensive scrutiny since the public bailout of private companies in 2008/9. As the leftish singer Billy Bragg has said, interviewed in the centre-right *Financial Times*, this is the age of accountability.

How do we hold to account, for instance, the world's largest investment management company Black Rock, who in 2013 controlled US$14.1 trillion directly traded assets and US$11 trillion assets overseas? US$15 trillion are traded on its Aladdin platform, which is the equivalent of 7% of all shares held worldwide, through 17,000 traders. Black Rock controls 5% of twenty of the largest capitalised companies. Its success and survival strategy has been to spread its risk across multiple companies and markets. The total assets traded worldwide by all investment companies in 2013 were valued at US$225 trillion.[9]

John Bridge Aspinall is buried in Bath Abbey, England. He died on 3rd May 1850 and his headstone says he was 'an active magistrate, beneficent to fellow creatures, kind to his family and just to all'. The only problem with this epitaph is: although there is still a plaque in the abbey, Aspinall made his fortune out of slavery. Although it's still prevalent in the twenty-first century, slavery was made illegal in the UK and colonies in 1833 and in the USA in 1865. This business, like many others, no longer gains approval from society but prospered from the fifteenth to the nineteenth centuries and the African slave trade is reckoned to have killed some 18,000,000 people, quite apart from the millions who were transported. At today's rate (based on 1950 and compared with WWII), this would be equivalent of 83,000,000 deaths against WWII at 55,000,000. Yet

9 *The Economist*, 7 December 2013: 13, 25-27.

we recognise and lament the latter, but not yet the former.[10] Today the Global Slavery Index calculates that there are about 30,000,000 slaves worldwide, nearly half living in India.[11]

Slavery is no longer acceptable at the institutional level even if it is still very much practised, albeit covertly. Similarly, progress has been made in other areas of human evolution and learning such as child labour, gender inequality, workplace health and safety, and racism although in many countries abuse in these areas is still endemic, and in some cases things are going backwards. But technological and therefore social change is exponentially much more rapid than ever. Will it slow down?

Bourke is a lyrical place, despite its name, and was made infamous by the poet Henry Lawson who wrote that 'if you know Bourke you know Australia', which, given its role in the late nineteenth and early twentieth centuries as a hub of the wool industry, was certainly true then. The town of Bourke is one of many that history has created and passed by, leaving an empty heart and one of the highest crime rates in Australia. But, in 1900, some 50% of the world's wool passed through it on the Darling River. To stand by the river now watching the mobs of rosellas and lorikeets flashing downstream and back again, apparently aimlessly, is to imagine a world of intense industry.

It is said that Australia's current wealth was founded on the back of the sheep. Bourke was the gateway to the bush: a major trading post and a logistics centre. The transformation now, just one hundred years later, is a lesson in change. Today agricultural products amount to single figures in Australia's export earnings and the sector employs less than 2% of all jobs in Australia.

10 Pinker, *Better Angels of our Nature*: 195.
11 www.globalslaveryindex.org, accessed 11 August 2014.

The growth industry for the last few decades has been mining. Sheep and cattle farming with their cloven, clodhopping hooves disturbed the delicate thin topsoil of Australia. Such farming was and still is unsuitable for that terrain and geology. Now, it is the lithosphere that is being mined; on the back of this the economy has boomed for the last twenty years. Australia is comparatively egalitarian and the historical strength of the trade unions means that it has one of the highest minimum wages in the world: Australia's minimum wage is a living wage. In the two decades to 2014 all socioeconomic classes have got richer, something that is true nowhere else in the world over the same period.

The first fleet arrived with a few sheep in 1788, but it wasn't until the next century that the wool trade took off following the introduction of sheep suitable to Australia's climate and geography. At the first auction of Australian wool in London in 1821 a kilo fetched $2.27. By the 1930s Australia was reliant on the wool trade with some 62% of primary product income coming from the back of the sheep.

Today natural fibres have become popular again, both for aesthetic and allergy-awareness reasons. Wool prices are as high as they've ever been, and sheep farmers who have managed to cope with both drought and feed issues are making a killing in this market. Today wool is a high-end product and the poor wear synthetic derivatives, but in 1900 wool and cotton comprised the basis of most clothing worldwide for rich and poor.

Since 1900, sheep farming has become heavily mechanised and agriculture generally provides very few jobs per dollar earned. Australia has strong tourist and higher education income sectors but it relies heavily for its national wealth on supplying minerals and fossil fuels all over the world, particularly to its primary markets in China, Japan and South Korea. In many ways the Australian economy has always relied on exporting raw materials to the world and this remains true today. It is one of the richest countries in the world, in terms of per capita income, but this is predicated on the world continuing to want its products. The demand for cheap power for electricity means that Australia's fossil fuel, in particular, will remain in demand for at least five to ten years, but it may have to become a more creative and innovative economy adding value at source in the years to come.

It is very much a nineteenth- or twentieth-century economy operating in the twenty-first century. Australian journalist, writer, social critic and academic Donald Horne said in 1964 that it was 'the lucky country, run by second rate people who share its luck'. He meant that it showed a lack of enterprise and innovation, and its luck included being a democracy: its luck also derived from inheriting, or stealing, its resources from the Indigenous population and inheriting a parliamentary system from Britain. In the twenty-first century it scores well on most social indicators despite its media being significantly controlled by Rupert Murdoch's empire and its politics being driven by the mining sector.

Finance as empire

I cite slavery and wool production as two examples of the creative destruction and social disruption that accompanies capitalism. The industrial revolution, originating in Great Britain in the mid eighteenth century and then rapidly taken up across Europe, changed the course, shape and destiny of humankind and its relationship to the Earth. Britain's dramatic colonisation had up to that point been horizontal, but the mining of the lithosphere heralded a vertical colonisation that continues more than two hundred years later with the mining of fossil fuel and mineral deposits laid down over the previous four billion years.

The release of these resources for human consumption has changed irrevocably every manner of human endeavour, every aspect of human relationship, and every day for ever, with one very significant caveat: humans forget their evolutionary past at our peril. We are still, for all our scientific and technological advances, the accumulation of the learnings, evolutions and adaptations that have happened to us over the millions of years. We must also not forget, in our rush to adopt new technologies, that we are physically and consciously part of the universe – as the emerging sciences of cosmology and physics are increasingly telling us and as the ancient philosophies of many Indigenous cultures have foretold.

My grandmother died aged 97 some years ago having lived through most of the twentieth century. Others have written of the relatively glacial changes of the period up to the industrial revolution when one generation could expect much the same as the previous in terms of lifestyle, life expectation, work and weather patterns. In the twentieth century Rachel Carson described 'the rapidity and the speed with which new situations are created' which 'follow the heedless pace of man rather than the deliberate pace of nature'. My grandmother would have agreed. In her lifetime she had seen two world wars, the bombing of Hiroshima and Nagasaki, the internal combustion engine, plumbing and toilets brought inside, penicillin, radio, TV, the internet, flight, people walking on the Moon, the first pictures of Earth from space, sliced white bread, obesity becoming a pandemic, corn syrup, and the progress from horse shit to air pollution caused by the internal combustion engine. She used to talk about how she and my grandfather used to collect the dung from Barnet Hill in North London for their vegetable gardens.

As we log on to social media, or pull the chain in the toilet, or drive a car down the highway, or vote online, we must remember how far we have come in the development of the systems that support everyday human life. Many innovations in power structure developments culminated in democratic developments in Europe in the nineteenth century, and these have now fanned out across the world. The evolution of participation by all, for all, at all times, and on all issues has been accompanied by dramatic revolutions and wars, and the fall of dynasties, dictatorships and despots. This evolutionary adaptation has been accompanied by, and limited and controlled by, industrial capitalism, and, now, in the twenty-first century, by global social media. The end of the Second World War saw the birth of welfare capitalism where the state, particularly in Europe, Canada, Australia and New Zealand, sought to distribute wealth and provide significant social safety nets as well civilising these countries with the abolition of the death penalty and strict gun control. These measures have also been adopted by newly democratised countries such as Japan but have not been adopted to anything like the same extent in countries like the USA, Brazil and Russia.

In the mid 1970s, another revolution took place which saw the service industries, such as finance and information technology, becoming central to a country's economic fortunes. Accompanying this focus was a second wave of globalisation, the first wave having happened during the nineteenth century and generally thought to have contributed to the two world wars. As these wars led to the creation of the Bretton Woods institutions, so the 1970s saw a move away from the central role of government in managing the economy and the introduction of neoliberalism with its central and fundamentalist belief in the rationality of the market. It did not mean a reduced role for the state, but it did lead to its role changing from wealth provider and wealth distributor to wealth enabler and market regulator. It saw information, choice and consumerism as drivers of innovation and wealth creation and allowed financial institutions to develop products that made money from money rather than wealth being made by innovations in value creation.

The money revolution was led in the UK by Margaret Thatcher's Big Bang in the London financial markets and in the USA by Ronald Reagan's project of exporting neoliberal economic policies as part and parcel of the selling of democracy. Democracy was not seen as a good in itself but as a way of enabling markets to operate. This was a specific twist to capitalism which has given us today a world awash with cash but with little moral or social responsibility about or control of the creation of wealth. In today's world, investment chases the lowest costs whether they be financial, environmental or social. This models cares not for the *political* economy, just for financial profit at all costs. Because a majority of the cash is institutional, we are all bound to its logic because it is our shareholdings, pension funds and property values that are tied to this race to the bottom. All those who are in for a penny are in for a pound: we are all complicit because we cannot divorce or disconnect ourselves from its inherent logic.

And so it was that when the engines of the global economies at the heart of the democracies, the world's banks, went bust in 2008/9 they had to be bailed out because they were us and we were them, indivisible. The banks were too big to fail, for if they failed we all failed; the whole edifice of the current model of capitalism would come crashing down around us and we would be back to the great depression of the 1930s – which had led to the Second World War.

But crucially it was not capitalism, but this particular model of capitalism, and the men and women of the corporations that operated it, that are to blame for this spectacularly unstable global political economy. As John Lanchester has said, in his many books on capitalism in the twenty-first century, most of us do not understand how the system works despite the fact that our lives are inextricably linked to it:

> I know all about this type of semi-knowledge, because I was that person. Now that I know more about it, I think everybody else should too. Just as CP Snow said that everyone should know the second law of thermodynamics, everyone should know about interest rates, and why they matter, and also what monetarism is, and what GDP is, and what an inverted yield curve is, and why it's scary. From that starting point, of language, we begin to have the tools to make up an economic picture, or pictures. Money is a lot like babies, and once you know the language, the rule is the same as that put forward by Dr Spock: 'Trust yourself, you know more than you think you do.'[12]

A brief history of capitalism – as I have noted, a word never used by Adam Smith in any of his writings – shows that the word only came into use in the 1860s and in particular after the publication in 1867 of Karl Marx's *Das Kapital*. The foundations of the origins of the idea of capitalism were the division of labour, the British industrial revolution in the mid eighteenth century and the democratic revolution in France in 1789. The

12 Lanchester, 'How to speak money'.

industrial revolution provided increased access to the Earth's resources and raw materials and the technology to exploit them, and the French revolution created the idea of an emancipated population but also an emancipated consumer class increasingly able to make political and economic choices. Economic wealth sprang from the industrial revolution, first in Britain, then in Germany, and then across the whole of Europe and to the USA. Its principles were that wealth flowed from competitive private enterprise, which, bursting free from previously feudal conditions, created an immediate bonanza for many, via the following precepts: buy in a cheap market (including labour), and sell in a dearer market; financial risk takers should keep the profits and thereby would become the *nouvelle riche*, the bourgeoisie, and, if everyone took risks equally, wealth would be distributed among all; the state would, through rules and regulations, guarantee property rights and profit taking; and civil rights and democracy were permitted as long they didn't impinge on or restrict the risk–reward basis of capitalism.[13]

The development of a particular model of capitalism from the mid nineteenth century until 1945 and then from 1945 until about the mid 1970s was further enabled by distanced, and disinterested, investment and management through the introduction of limited liability first in France and then by statute in 1855 in the British parliament.

Friedrich Hayek, Thatcher and Reagan's guide and mentor with his fellow travellers in which is known as the Chicago School, said: 'It is of the utmost importance . . . to keep in mind that the planning against which all our criticism is directed is solely planning against competition' but there is 'the very

13 See Eric Hobsbawm, *The Age of Revolution. Europe: 1789–1848* (London: Abacus, 1962); *The Age of Capital: 1848–1875* (London: Weidenfeld & Nicolson, 1975).

necessary planning which is required to make competition as effective and beneficial as possible'.[14] In other words, as Margaret Thatcher discovered, this does not necessarily mean small government, but rather rules and processes that facilitate competition in all spheres of life, that commoditise and marketise all aspects of society, where all decisions are seen as essentially economic and transactional. This ideology is based on the fundamental and profound misconception that markets are both rational and moral: that they deliver outcomes that benefit all. A mixture of markets, trade, cooperation, social cohesion and collaboration certainly produce socially beneficial outcomes but market mechanisms that resist other features certainly do not produce the good society.

Managing a socially just market economy with requisite freedoms and human rights provisions requires the management of uncertainty and complexity, as well as flexibility, and these features may be beyond the abilities of the average politician, and are certainly beyond the capacities of a politician ideologically glued to a particular creed. It is fine to have a clear vision and set of transparent values but this is not the same as dogmatism. The legislative frameworks left in place by Thatcher in the UK and Ronald Reagan in the USA in the 1970s and '80s were no less in their prescriptiveness than more balanced economies, but they were biased towards division, competition and winner-takes-all. In the case of Pinochet's Chile, the imposition of the same ideological fanaticism required the suppression of democracy and dissent and the 'disappearance' of some 30,000 people.

Adam Smith, often described as 'the father of modern capitalism', a description he would probably have run from, wrote

14 Hayek, *The Road to Serfdom*: 45.

with a very different world-view from today's.[15] Indeed, as others have pointed out, his world was boundless and the idea of frontier capitalism obvious, for most people had not yet reached the other side of the world. What world? Where did it end? Indeed, he would probably have understand the idea of valuing what are now known as environmental services and what are also known as the five capitals: environmental, social, human, built and financial. This what Smith said:

> [The rich] consume little more than the poor, and in spite of their natural selfishness and rapacity . . . they divide with the poor the produce of all their improvements. They are led by an invisible hand to make nearly the same distribution of the necessaries of life, which would have been made, had the earth been divided into equal portions among all its inhabitants, and thus without intending it, without knowing it, advance the interest of the society, and afford means to the multiplication of the species.[16]

> Every individual . . . neither intends to promote the public interest, nor knows how much he is promoting it . . . he intends only his own security; and by directing that industry in such a manner as its produce may be of the greatest value, he intends only

15 'If anybody bothered to read Adam Smith they'd see he pointed out that social policy is class based. He took the class analysis for granted' (Noam Chomsky, 'The New Global Economy' [interview with David Barsamian], Third World Traveler; www.thirdworldtraveler.com/Chomsky/ChomOdon_GlobEcon.html, accessed 16 December 2014; from Noam Chomsky, *The Prosperous Few and the Restless Many* [Tucson, AZ: Odonian Press, 1993]).
16 Adam Smith, *The Theory of Moral Sentiments* (1759): Book IV, Chapter I, Para 10.

> his own gain, and he is in this, as in many other
> cases, led by an invisible hand to promote an end
> which was no part of his intention.[17]

Smith wrote in a society where most people knew each other, where human networks were not so diffuse. It is most important to note that, at the time he was writing, the class system and wealth division were seen as natural and God-given. There is no part of his writing that expects the accepted social structure to change. His is not the economics of liberation, class struggle or social mobility. It is the economics of mercantilism and trade. He was writing as a moral political economist within a narrow definition of society, not as a disinterested rationalist, and that is the mistake that many who now follow him fail to grasp. He did not think that unintentional selfishness, the heartbeat of neoliberal economics, would help us all – it would increase trade and maintain the social order.

Capitalism and economics did not fail in the 2008/9 crash because capitalism and economics has no memory, soul or conscience. It is simply an idea given substance by its political context. It was that context that failed then and continues to fail now. The dominant model of economics that dominates many large national economies and international trade and banking is illusory, but, in the eyes of commentators such as Philip Mirowski, the logic of the neoliberalists is that the market 'is the ultimate information system'. It is omnipotent and superior to human intelligence and *should*, like god, be beyond our control because, if we dally with it, it will fail us. Mirowski, Yvonne Roberts, Piketty and others observe that this model, which espouses freedom through liberalisation, marketisation,

17 Adam Smith, *An Inquiry into the Nature and Causes of the Wealth of Nations* (1776): Book IV, Chapter 2, Para. 9.

commodification and objectification, has enslaved us all by quantifying all human activity only in financial terms. It would have us trade every tree, all the Earth's resources and our love for one another in worship of the market.[18] It has infantilised us all in the pursuit of the false god of financial growth.

According to Mirowski, business and management schools have been factories for the production of the managers of profit maximisation and the growth of the corporate body. And when the private body goes belly-up, the public state, which under neoliberalism should wither away, is supposed to bail it out, so enmeshed is the state with the pursuit of private profit. The triumph of capitalism since 1945 is the triumph of freedom, accountability, collective strength, enterprise and innovation, not the triumph of free markets. But in the last forty years the former has been closely allied to the latter. However, the evidence is that, unless markets, enterprise and freedom are closely allied to accountability, good governance, the rule of law, mutuality, and recognition of the intrinsic value and rights of labour and the Earth, it fails. Where business and management schools – and, indeed, departments of economics – have been most useful is where they have been interdisciplinary and non-fundamentalist and understood that managing the *political* economy is about managing complexity. And this is so different from managing the comparative simplicity of the single

18 Philip Mirowski, *Never Let a Serious Crisis Go to Waste: How Neoliberalism Survived the Financial Meltdown* (London/New York: Verso Books, 2013); Yvonne Roberts, 'In the Public Interest: The Role of The Modern State' (London: The Centre for Labour and Social Studies [Class]; classonline.org.uk/docs/2014_The_role_of_the_state_-_Yvonne_Roberts_FINAL.pdf, 2014); Thomas Piketty, *Capital in the Twenty-first Century* (Boston, MA: Harvard University Press, 2014).

bottom line: that is, for accountants, not for the art of political science and the good society.

Global surveys of trust show that people trust NGOs most, followed by business next and government last, but that they trust business *people* least. Indeed, paradoxically, they blame business people rather than the capitalist *system* or corporations for the collapse of global finances in 2008/9 and think that government should be doing more to control banking excesses and force business to be more honest, accountable and transparent.

Very few surveys show that people understand the inherent structural imbalances and lunacies of the current model of capitalism. This is probably because they are too complex to be understood by anyone, and too complicated for most people to begin to understand the arcaneries, subtle shifts and minutiae in the flow of money, services and goods around the world. If the majority of children in advanced democracies think milk is made in the back of the supermarket, how are most people going to understand derivatives, sub-primes and collaterals?

Colin Crouch points out, along with others, that one of the modern media myths perpetrated by neoliberalists and their wealthy financial supporters is the idea of the nanny state.[19] This is strange, as business tells us what to think, eat and do all the time through its marketing. It is also strange and contradictory because we are supposed to believe in the apparent efficiency of the private sector as opposed to the inefficiency of the public sector. There is so much evidence to ridicule let alone refute the idea that private management is efficient and public management is inefficient that it is difficult to know where to start. But: 80–90% of all hedge funds fail; the *pri-*

19 Colin Crouch, *The Strange Non-death of Neoliberalism* (Cambridge, UK: Polity Press, 2011).

vatised UK nuclear industry is run by the French *state-owned* EDF; the US's GM and the UK's RBS both had to be bailed out by their respective governments; the third largest supermarket group in the UK (by floorspace), The Co-op, is a cooperative, and one of the most successful retails groups, The John Lewis Group, is employee-owned; 25% of British railways have been 'privatised' and are now run by European governments. And Gazprom in Russia, SINOPEC in China and Medibank in Australia are all run as state-owned enterprises rather efficiently.

The Mont Pelerin Society, named after the Swiss town in which it first met in 1947, is dedicated to promoting neoliberalism – making a specific link between democracy and free-market economics: the freer the market, the more democratic a country. Its founding members included most of the Chicago School of economists, Friedrich Hayek, Milton Friedman, the Institute for Economic Affairs, Atlas, the Stockholm Network, and the Murdoch empire. The group's aims directly link free speech and economic freedom and they find it 'difficult to imagine a society in which freedom may be effectively preserved' without the 'diffused power and initiative' associated with 'private property and the competitive market'.[20]

We have all been forced to internalise the neoliberal logic that there is no other way: we have been subverted. If, as neoliberals argue, the market rules and is rational, it follows that, as we are all flawed (being humans), we should therefore be obeisant to the market. As a flawed human being, all my failures are personal; therefore all my market failures are mine. Even any belief I might have in a god or a spirit world is superficial when compared to the apparent rationality of the market;

20 https://www.montpelerin.org/montpelerin/mpsGoals.html, accessed 6 October 2014. See also Crouch, *The Strange Non-death of Neoliberalism.*

the market is a higher god than emotion, aesthetics, wisdom, spirituality or intuition.[21] This led Margaret Thatcher in 1987 to question the idea of society per se. What she actually said is: 'Who is society? There is no such thing! There are individual men and women and there are families and no government can do anything except through people and people look to themselves first.'[22] This is all very well, but relies on the notion that in 'looking to yourself first' you have the good of others in mind, visibly or invisibly. Was Thatcher thinking morally or just of individual rationalism? Or, as the supporters who reference Adam Smith say, was she arguing that individual

21 Michel Foucault, 'Key Concepts', www.michel-foucault.com/ concepts, accessed 5 December 2014; Mirowski, *Never Let a Serious Crisis Go to Waste.*

22 Margaret Thatcher said: 'I think we have gone through a period when too many children and people have been given to understand "I have a problem, it is the Government's job to cope with it!" or "I have a problem, I will go and get a grant to cope with it!" "I am homeless, the Government must house me!" and so they are casting their problems on society and who is society? There is no such thing! There are individual men and women and there are families and no government can do anything except through people and people look to themselves first. It is our duty to look after ourselves and then also to help look after our neighbour and life is a reciprocal business and people have got the entitlements too much in mind without the obligations, because there is no such thing as an entitlement unless someone has first met an obligation and it is, I think, one of the tragedies in which many of the benefits we give, which were meant to reassure people that if they were sick or ill there was a safety net and there was help, that many of the benefits which were meant to help people who were unfortunate – "It is all right . . ."' (www.margaretthatcher.org/document/106689, accessed 2 December 2014).

rationalism leads inevitably to the good society, bypassing the idea of the caring society?

My experience, and the evidence produced by Richard Wilkinson and Kate Pickett in *The Spirit Level*,[23] is that many people look to their community first because they know that that is where their security lies. A good example of this is a direct comparison between Britain and Japan. In Britain in 2014, the differential between the top and the bottom wages is now as high as it was in 1900: 175. In Japan, that difference would be abhorrent and antithetical to idea of the nation being one community – it would be politically unacceptable. But Britain is not one nation and is more akin to a network of nested tribal groups: north and south; private and state-educated; rich and poor; landed and housing-poor; urban and rural. Australia has similar divides except with a far more egalitarian culture and fairer wealth distribution. In Australia, over the twenty-year economic boom period to 2013, every socioeconomic group got richer as the tide lifted everyone, apart from Indigenous people.

The biggest problem with neoliberalism and its baggage – monetarism and liberalisation – is that its simplistic notions fail to deal with the complexities of life and existence. It is as fundamentally flawed and unrelated to empirical evidence as creationism and a belief in fairies (which I believe in, by the way, when I'm lying on my back in the long grass on a warm day listening to the skylarks calling above). It is so good to have a single thought that maintains all, that takes you forward day-to-day. The idea that the rationality of the market solves all is so wonderfully liberating. If only it were how life is.

23 Richard Wilkinson and Kate Pickett, *The Spirit Level: Why Equality is Better for Everyone* (London: Penguin, 2010).

Today we give away our thoughts for free and they are commoditised, for this is how much social media companies like Facebook, Twitter and LinkedIn operate, and how modern capitalist corporations like Amazon, Tesco and Google know what, where, how and when you do what you do all the time. They are watching, overtly and covertly. We are all entrapped and entranced and distracted so we don't complain, and most of the time we don't understand. When, on rare occasions, we do see Occupy and the Arab awakening, and, in the UK, anti-Poll Tax demonstrations, the forces of the neoliberal state send in their dogs and police with riot shields.

The fundamentals of capitalism are sound: the rule of law (or contract); reward for hard work and risk; and retaining the gains of our hard work and risk which sometimes means property rights. The problems we have to deal with are correcting markets when they go wrong – because they do – and dealing with those people who would seek power and massive wealth over all others through using and abusing markets and the agents of capitalism – government and corporations.

Modern communications technologies combined with the role of finance have made information a key commodity. Neoliberalism is now about information flow. If that is thought of as a flowing river, the river is now so fast, vast and furious that it cannot be stopped: we can merely build bigger dykes. In 2008/9 the river meandered and flooded out lives, threatening to drown us all. But the neoliberal state stepped in and private debt became public debt in apparent seamlessness.

To continue the analogy, 71% of the surface of the planet is covered in water, and so now the world is awash with financial capital looking for a return. This has come about since the introduction of neoliberalism in the 1970s and in particular since the liberalisation of the UK international banking system (the world's largest) with the support of Margaret Thatcher and Ronald Reagan and the theoretical underpinning of Friedrich Hayek and Chicago economics. Between 1970 and 1990, most capital changed from following trade and long-term investment to chasing short-term return.[24] This race to the bottom and to instant wealth creation has been mirrored in all aspects of life: chasing instant celebrity status, instant gratification via social media, obesity through constant grazing. Where is the time to stand and stare? Who is thinking of passing social and environmental capital on to our children's children?

I wrote about the accumulation of wealth and the development of the 99/1% wealth distribution in post-industrial societies earlier when discussing globality and Earth awareness, and I described how this led to the Occupy movement and other outpourings of resentment on a global basis. Just as religious fundamentalism, nationalism, tribalism and misogyny seem to fuel (and be based on) fear, hatred and violence of one group against another, so neoliberalism has produced similar enmities. But neoliberal capitalism is more hidden and mysterious. The post-WWII effort to distribute universal human rights, the rule of law, accountability and universal welfare safety nets internationally, which formed a civilising uniformity based on complex values supported by all members of the UN (and not just the West, as some have suggested), has been undermined by neoliberal logic and postcolonial anger. The

24 'In 1970, about 90% of international capital was used for trade and long-term investment – more or less productive things – and 10% for speculation. By 1990 those figures had reversed' (Noam Chomsky, 'Toward Greater Inequality' [interview with David Barsamian], Third World Traveler; www.thirdworldtraveler.com/Chomsky/ChomOdon_Inequality.html, accessed 16 December 2014; from Chomsky, *The Prosperous Few*).

current situation sees a clash of fundamentalism between, on the one hand, an inclusive model of social development based on celebrating diversity and secularism within a fundamental framework of common rights and obligations, and on the other hand the continued push for freedom to mean marketisation and financialisation.

The war against the Bretton Woods institutions and Keynesianism started in the 1970s and should have ended in 2008/9 with a clarion call for the public rectification of private capital manipulation. Instead, we have not only continued with a corrupt and flawed system but the financial world has climbed back out of the swamp and assumed the mountain tops. And the greatest warriors for this resumption of business-as-usual are those who have gained most from it: the 1% and those embedded in the senior levels of the world's best clubs – the supraterritorial corporations (STCs). Given the fragility of the system, the fast-flowing river of information, most democratically elected governments are in thrall and beholden to the STCs.

We need to understand that we have reached this point because of public policy decisions that have been made, mostly on our behalf. Our economic system is not like this because the market knows all, but because we have asked it to give us information which relates to a particular view of the world, in particular a very narrow view of wealth that includes a poor view of social capital and social welfare and zero understanding of environmental health. Ben Zander, author, composer and conductor, challenges us all: 'what assumptions have I made today that I don't know I've made?'[25] John Lanchester

25 Rosamund Zander and Benjamin Zander, *The Art of Possibility: Transforming Professional and Personal Life* (Boston, MA: Harvard Business School Press, 2000); see also 'The Art of Possibility:

says that we have not yet met the 'severe tests' of meeting 'the intellectual challenge' of our economic assumptions: how did we create the regulated entities that we now live under?[26]

The next section discusses how we came to this point where the STCs effectively rule and what can be done to regain control: to input greater levels of accountability and transparency into the world of global, rather than international, institutions that we are all inevitably drawn to like moths to the light. We are currently mining the lithosphere and ourselves, and we will either burn out or transcend this madness and ascend to a higher way of being. Just as it took the First and Second World Wars in Europe before we decolonised and saw the need for universal human rights and obligations and social welfare safety nets, will it take a further collapse of corporations and this model of capitalism for us to wake up and smell the future? I argue in this book that the changes are already under way, but we could give the inevitable a shove in the right direction.

Let's discuss political economy: corporate social responsibility and corporate citizenship are dead ends

It's been called the perfect storm. Population grows; wealth creates exponential resource depletion; and our asocial economic model relies on growth, resource exploitation and money as

---

Transforming Professional and Personal Life', Harvard Business School Working Knowledge; hbswk.hbs.edu/archive/1898.html, accessed 16 December 2014.

26 John Lanchester, 'What's Your Position on Octopus?', *Financial Times*, 30–31 August 2014: 3.

the root, rather than the servant, of all wealth creation; and our banks and corporate entities are the dominant institutions alongside necessary but outmoded nation-states.

The greatest challenges to change are the current economic system, nationalism, tribalism (in which is included religious fundamentalist churches) and misogyny. The clash of civilisations is between those who understand that we have one world, finite resources, limited lifespans and a beautiful world, and those who believe in the infinite exploitation of people, planet and resources for personal, national or tribal gain. For some, this situation is best summed up as an Earth- and human-centric model of political economy versus neoliberal economics.

In Chapter 1 I discussed the age of globality and Earth awareness, where interdependence is the natural *modus operandi*, and in Chapter 2 I discussed the fact that peace is breaking out. Both of these major social systems changes in the history of humanity require three things to happen: individuals to act as local and global citizens; new global governance institutions; and new management skills and expertise to be taught in schools and universities.

Our global economic system needs new rules, and not *no* rules; and our supra-territorial corporations, whether state-, mutually or shareholder-owned, need new rules on governance, transparency, responsibility, rights, reporting and accountability. So, how did we get to this state?

Let's distinguish between two issues. First, we all believe in markets, exchange and trade. Who wouldn't? Second, it is recognised that society is made up of institutions and organisations. Both are made in our own image, but both are now in need of rigorous examination to see if they deliver public and social good and to see if they conform to the principle of 'do no harm' and 'the precautionary principle'.

Throughout this book I have tried to bring the arguments down to Earth, and here is another brief grounding. As one of those who helped give birth to the Farmers' Market movement in the UK in the 1990s – a return to the principle of face-to-face trade and real markets – last Saturday at Bath Farmers' Market I was able to discuss the merits and ingredients of spelt (an ancient, low-gluten flour) bread with a local baker and ask a farmer when her carrots were lifted that morning and what fertiliser she had used to grow them. My exchanges were accompanied by informed discussion and a few laughs – and, what's most important, looking each other in the eye. For our lives to be more than simple transactional reckonings, all markets, exchange and trade should be imbued with value creation and a sense of a greater worth: the value that supports William Wordsworth's inner eye and Rachel Carson's sense of the whole. A full human life is based on love, laughter and learning – and beauty. Shopping should be a joyous experience – it is, after all, as central to all our lives as eating, drinking and sleeping.

A very brief look at dates helps in understanding the evolution of global trade from the local market to the modern corporation, an institution that now dominates all our lives.

In 1600, a Royal Charter established the British East India Company with a purview to trade on behalf of Britain to the east of the Cape of Good Hope in South Africa and west of the Straits of Magellan. Much European expansionism was predicated on trade, and on trading companies with guns and bibles following up to 'civilise' people and markets. In 1776 – while the industrial revolution had barely begun – Adam Smith published *The Wealth of Nations* drawing on both theory and practice around the world. The eighteenth century saw the start of the industrial revolution; the Joint Stock Companies

Act (UK) of 1844 and the Limited Liability Act (UK) of 1855 (France had been first a few years earlier in this regard) provided the basis for the modern company. The Joint Stock Companies Act 1856 (UK) followed and the modern corporation was born: limited liability, disinterested investments, overseas management, and a management class operating for investors – and often, as has been noted, for themselves.

The corporation is an extraordinary vehicle for the creation of more prosperity and misery than could ever be imagined. For many, it is seen as a law unto itself which threatens to eat us alive. Many global corporations are so large, and so complex, that they are almost beyond reckoning – and certainly out of control. The corporation is a legal fiction – a bizarre creation which under the law passes as an individual, whereas of course it lacks body, soul and mind.

The corporate responsibility industry, of which I have been a part from some twenty-five years, has been attempting to bring the corporation into line by introducing accountability, governance and reporting measures; but these are really only playing at the edges. As former UBS director Colin Mayer says in *Firm Commitment*, 'We are trying to control the whale by tickling its tail . . . there have been serious deficiencies in both the efficient delivery of public goods and services, and the effective adherence of corporations to responsible conduct.'[27] Norwegian-born French judge Eva Joly, charged with investigating large French corporations, said in an interview in 2014 that corporations represented a 'new form of colonialism'. In this she echoed Rachel Carson's sense of outrage – cited earlier – at the irresponsibility of chemical companies in the 1950s and

27 Colin Mayer, *Firm Commitment: Why the corporation is failing us and how to restore trust in it* (Oxford, UK: Oxford University Press, 2013): 4, 10.

'60s who put dangerous chemicals in the hands of salespeople and farmers who did not fully understand the consequences of their sales and use.[28]

In a book written in 1992 for the then recently formed (World) Business Council for Sustainable Development (a rival to the emergent UN Global Compact), WBCSD's founder Stephan Schmidheiny touched on the core problem with the link between markets and corporations:

> If markets really do encourage efficient resource use and decreases in pollution, then we must ask ourselves why the past record of industrialization is largely one of unsustainable resource use and high levels of pollution . . . The most effective pursuit of sustainable development is 'getting the price right' . . . Unless prices for raw materials and products properly reflect the social costs . . . Resources will tend to be used inefficiently and environmental pollution will increase.[29]

The main vehicle for the expansion of global markets and the financialisation of all aspects of life has been through the corporation, particularly through banks. Those that work for them, particularly at a senior management level, have become the foot soldiers and the prime beneficiaries of a system that serves them and some shareholders well but does not deliver social and environmental goods. If it does, it is unintentional, for it is not the main mission of the corporation to care about

28 Eva Joly on BBC Radio 4, interviewed by Helena Kennedy QC, 19 August 2014, 09.00.
29 Stephan Schmidheiny and the Business Council for Sustainable Development (1992) *Changing Course: A Global Business Perspective on Development and the Environment* (Cambridge, MA: MIT Press): 15-17.

society, communities or the planet. And it can never be under the current rules. Just as Hitler's lieutenants were able to argue at the Nuremburg trials that they were merely carrying out orders, so too Carson's chemical salesmen in the 1960s and now and sub-prime mortgage purveyors in the twenty-first century were just doing their jobs, whether in the UK or the USA or elsewhere.

At present, corporations are capitalised and valued as such; but, as many have said, they should be valued on what they do, not on what they are nominally worth on the stock market. As Colin Mayer has said:

> The goals of the economically efficient provision of goods and services, technological innovation, and employment creation (*through the corporation*) are not achieved by arrangements that confer property rights on one party and protect others inadequately through contracts and public law.[30]

A corporation, albeit a legal 'person', cannot knowingly do harm – only its officers can know, and they are merely agents for the owners who in most cases are so distanced as to be over the horizon and far away. Unless we change the laws governing incorporation, limited liability and corporate malfeasance, corporations, whether they are shareholder- or state-owned, will continue to rape and pillage in their interests just as marauding Vikings and Mongols did centuries before.

Corporations are our servants and operate by our rules. It is for us to change the rules. They work on market rules that are in urgent need of updating to make transparent the hidden connections between how they make money and their social and environmental impact. This cannot simply be left to laggardly

30 Mayer, *Firm Commitment*: 259.

public bodies, weak states and citizens' movements: we must change the very operating rules on which corporations survive.

Peter Drucker died in 2005 after more than sixty years of writing on business and management. Just as this book has invited the re-reading of Darwin, Carson, Hutton, Lovelock, Smith and many others, so there is merit in reiterating Drucker's thinking:

> Profitability is not the purpose of, but a limiting factor on business enterprise and business activity. Profitability is not the explanation, cause or rationale of business behaviour or decisions, but rather a test of their validity.[31]

> Business enterprises – and public-service institutions as well – are organs of society. They do not exist for their own sake, but to fulfill a specific purpose and to satisfy a specific need of a society, a community, or individuals.[32]

This last point was made in 1973 – more than forty years ago. But at this time the revolution that was to be known as neoliberalism was nascent – an enormous misnomer as the term 'liberalism' has different connotations in the US, Europe and elsewhere.[33]

In 1973 Friedrich Hayek won the Nobel Prize for economics, and the Chicago School of economics was becoming dominant.

31 Peter F. Drucker, *Post Capitalist Society* (1999), in *The Essential Drucker*: 347.
32 Peter F. Drucker, *Concept of the Corporation* (Piscataway, NJ: Transaction Publishers, 1993 [1946]); *Management: Tasks, Responsibilities, Practices* (New York: HarperBusiness, 1993 [1973]): 16.
33 For an excellent unpacking of neoliberalism, see Crouch, *The Strange Non-death of Neoliberalism*.

In this same year Peter Drucker published *Management: Tasks, Responsibilities, Practices*. After establishing the principles of 'the purpose and mission of the institution; making work productive and the worker effective' he said that 'the third task of management is managing the social impacts and responsibilities of the enterprise', because 'free enterprise cannot be justified as being good for business; it can be justified only as being good for society'. He was countering Milton Friedman, one of Hayek's closest co-fundamentalists and a member of both the Chicago school and the Mont Pelerin Society, who had said in 1970: 'There is one and only one social responsibility of business – to use it resources and engage in activities designed to increase its profits.'[34]

In 1973, Middle East countries ended the oil boycott of the US, Europe and Japan, which had heralded the first attempts at making the internal combustion engine more efficient, just a year after the world's first international environment conference in Stockholm in 1972. Ceefax starts! Remember that? And the first barcodes were used on Wrigley's chewing gum. Pepsico became the first US company to sell into the USSR (it was to remain a totalitarian 'communist' country for another 16 years).

It is the contention of many that it is large international corporations, and particularly the banks, that have kept alive the neoliberal mode of economics because they are part and parcel

34 'There is one and only one social responsibility of business – to use it resources and engage in activities designed to increase its profits so long as it stays within the rules of the game, which is to say, engages in open and free competition without deception or fraud' (Milton Friedman, 'The Social Responsibility of Business is to Increase its Profits', *New York Times Magazine*, 13 September 1970; www.umich.edu/~thecore/doc/Friedman.pdf).

of its fundamentalist cause. It is in their DNA that capital should race to the bottom, as in the sub-prime mortgage debacle, and as in the case of the 2013 Bangladesh clothing factory collapse in which more than 1,000 people died.[35] Of course, many who work for these companies – and we are all complicit in their existence and survival – plead their goodness and say that they are no more evil than corrupt officials in other areas of life. But the fact is that the vehicles they drive have wonky steering: they are set to drive us all into the ditch. It is all very well arguing for the innate goodness of individuals if they are working in and for institutions which are themselves set to be amoral.[36]

To repeat, in *Silent Spring* Rachel Carson pointed out that she wasn't opposed to the use of chemicals in farming, but she was opposed to their indiscriminate and irresponsible use and sales by people who knew not what they were selling. This is the Nuremburg defence and could be used by most people who work in large corporations:

> It is not my contention that chemical pesticides must never be used. I do contend that we have put poisonous and biologically potent chemicals indiscriminately into the hands of persons largely ignorant of their potentials for harm.[37]

35 Jason Burke, 'Rana Plaza: One Year On from the Bangladesh Factory Disaster', *The Guardian*, 19 April 2014; www.theguardian.com/world/2014/apr/19/rana-plaza-bangladesh-one-year-on, accessed 5 December 2014.

36 See Mark Moody-Stuart, 'Business as a Vocation', *Journal of Corporate Citizenship* 55 (September 2014): 9-12.

37 Carson, *Silent Spring*: 29.

The adjustment to the steering is both simple and very difficult because it requires coordinated global action based on a shared understanding that action is needed – and that point has still not arrived.

After more than forty years of the neoliberal experiment, and the financialisation of everything, we should be at the point where we join the dots and make the links between economics, climate change adaptation, population, resource scarcity and efficiency, and global governance. This requires systems thinking at the highest level and notions of responsible leadership that most political and business leaders are not capable of. The only solution is civil action from the street up to put pressure on all leaders to come to the party and stop the truck so that we do not end up in the ditch.

As trust in business and government falls to a real low point, the initiative must be seized by all those in quiet leadership positions to stop tinkering at the edges and to focus on changing the system. Peter Drucker said in 1973 that 'businesses are organs of society' and forty years later this is echoed by many, including Ben Boyd from Edelman, the global PR company: 'Today's world requires a shift from the historic, transactional nature of capitalism to a model of value creation that encompasses societal benefit as well as shareholder value . . . It's the responsibility of business to redefine and re-prioritize the way it thinks about value.'[38]

And I'm thinking of smelling the cheese at my local farmers' market before buying it, and discussing the cheese-maker's

---

38 'Trust in government plunges to historic low: Business trust stabilizes, creating largest gap ever between trust in government and business', Edelman press release, 19 January 2014; www.edelman.com/news/trust-in-government-plunges-to-historic-low, accessed 19 February 2014.

milk source, and wondering how to make that human-scale moment part of my everyday transactions – and the creation of real business value.

Reviving political economy

There are many idiocies in the financialisation of everything; but where water, energy and banking are concerned the insanity is most obvious. How is it that something as elementary and fundamental as water has come to be owned, bottled and sold back to us? And how is it that so many of the companies that now control water are state-owned and not marketised in the sense that Hayek envisaged? How is it that the banks, those monoliths of the 1980s deregulation, have had to be bailed out by the apparently loathed state? How is it that the UK taxpayer subsidises the French taxpayer to maintain the French state-owned enterprise EDF to keep monopoly control of all the UK's nuclear power industry? Lewis Carroll could not have conceived of such bizarre outcomes, but then this is the triumph and irony of planning that favours market solutions. How is it that we lambast energy companies but most of their resources are actually owned by governments, not by the companies that exploit those resources? The exploitation companies have a hold on public policy similar to the hold that slavery companies had in the nineteenth century and tobacco companies had in the twentieth century – and still do in some countries. And, as I have discussed, banking is propped up by the state, so close is the nexus. We need public policy and moral sanity to prevail.

One of the greatest lessons is that the history of all national expansions and local enterprise is a mix of public planning and policy allied with private risk and entrepreneurship. But, when the forces of private enterprise become too strong, the public purpose disappears. Chinese, Russian, Brazilian and Indonesian mercantilism in the twenty-first century today is a case in point.

Today, the financialisation of everything means that we can apparently only measure things we can count, so money becomes the only commodity. Neoliberalism measures all those things that can be counted and cares not for all those things that matter: community, social cohesion and neighbourliness. And it most definitely does not lead to an emancipated, empowered universal capitalist class.

We have become servants of neoliberalism. So too have we become servants of atomised science rather than systems thinking, despite the wealth of evidence that we should moving in the contrary direction. This is because thinking systems or systems thinking requires time, effort, reflection and a sense of awe, and these are all aspects of life that are too difficult for most people today. (Oh, yes, I must post that thought NOW on Twitter and update my Facebook page immediately – I had cornflakes for breakfast and my dog needs a shampoo.)

Similarly, a single bottom line is so much easier for the simple business mind than a complex map of interactions and connections, many of which are immeasurable but can only be felt, observed or dreamt about.

Hence the call by the UN High-Level Panel for a new model of political economy where disparate views are connected. Because, as the US/UK political economists Tony Judt and Timothy Snyder observed in *Thinking the Twentieth Century:*

> Money makes goods measurable. It blurs discussion as to their respective standing in an ethical or normative conversation about social purposes. I think it would serve us all well to 'kill all the economists'

(to paraphrase Shakespeare): very few of them add
to the sum of social or scientific knowledge, but a
substantial majority of the profession contributes
actively to confusing their fellow citizens about
how to think socially.[39]

Thomas Piketty's *Capital in the Twenty-first Century* may be
light on prescriptions, but his detailed and transparent analysis
of how wealth was created in the last century accords with
anthropologist David Graeber, both of whom would agree that
social mobility and shareholder democracy are only possible
if government is actively involved in *pre-* and *re*-distribution.
Markets, with their sole fixation on money, will not allow for
the imperfections and idiosyncrasies of society and communities. Therefore, I applaud Piketty's call for the resurrection of
political economy and the sublimation of the idea that economics is a science – as this has put us all in the ditch.

> I see economics as a subdiscipline of the social sci-
> ences, alongside history, sociology, anthropology,
> and political science . . . I much prefer the term
> 'political economy', which may seem rather old-
> fashioned, because what we are concerned with is
> 'political, normative, and moral purpose'.[40]

The new international political economy must be founded
on systems thinking and incorporate the five issues raised in
this book: globality and Earth awareness; rebalancing science
and awe; peacefulness and the feminisation of decision-making; reorganising our institutions and economics; and focusing
on the links between evolution, adaptation and learning.

39 Tony Judt with Timothy Snyder, *Thinking the Twentieth
   Century* (London: Vintage, 2012): 382.
40 Piketty, *Capital in the Twenty-first Century*: 574.

5

Quiet leadership: evolution, adaptation, learning

My boat ever drifts between mist and waves;

In a rock cave, I hung my cloud gourd, not know-
ing the meaning of this, what man is humming as
he collects driftwood.[1]

For two reasons this final chapter begins with a quotation from Kuncan, an abbot in a Chan Buddhist monastery, Nanjing, China, in 1666, The first is to re-emphasise the link between knowing, half-seeing and dreaming, and between the practicalities of life and theory. The second is to note again the development of different, but similar, cultures around the world. In the West we have tended to teach history from a Western

---

1 British Museum, 'Gems of Chinese Painting: A Voyage along the Yangzi River', London, 2014.

perspective without due recognition of worlds far away. Kun-can's reality is that of a recluse who drifts between a spiritual world and reality. This inscription accompanies a series of paintings by him for friend and peer Cheng Zhengkui; these are part of the British Museum's collection in London.

The theme of evolution, adaptation and learning lends itself to an addition to the transitions theme in Chapter 1 on glo-bality. I have pointed out that humans share one history, and it is obvious that they (we) share one planet. It also seems obvious that we forget our evolutionary past at our peril, so tied are we to fight or flight, to the need to keep warm, and to eat and drink often. We are soft-skinned, and our survival and evolution, adaptation and learning is based on sociabil-ity, social cohesion and understanding how society and socie-ties work. Our success at interaction, which is increasing and not decreasing as we evolve out more masculine characteristics and become more feminine, is on several different levels. The sociologist Pitirim Sorokin, writing in the 1930s, said that the idealistic harmonises the sensate and the ideational. He pointed out that the ideational tendency is to be found in all religions, East and West. These are the ideas of justice, fair play, reciproc-ity, accountability, truth and beauty.[2] He also thought that the world would become more peaceful as the idea of war, and its destruction of all values, would diminish.

The problem is not the sensate, the ideational or the idealistic but the subcultures of organisation, tribes, identity and belong-ing which have tended to set us against one another. Those who set up and lead these divisions are often driven by enmity and power lust rather than interaction, cohesion and a sense of one-ness. They live in the sensate world and use ideational goals to

2 See Capra, *The Turning Point*: 13.

drive people into tribal identity, whether that be national, corporate or sporting. The problems arise from fear of 'the other' and dipping into our reptilian evolutionary past.

Are we discussing utopias when we build the new political economy? John Carey's monumental compilation and analysis of utopias makes some salient points on this, which, in a sense go to the heart of this book's debate. First: is the idea of utopia, of some promised land, central to what it means to be human? That hope springs eternal. Second: are utopias individual or collective dreams? He points out that many utopian discussions are based on nature and reason and what constitutes reasonable behaviour. As he says, modern utopias often discuss issues such as feminism or euthanasia. Perhaps sustainability is today's utopia, and perhaps, as discussed earlier, sustainability is a product of an affluent mind, while neoliberalism is the counterweight dystopia.[3]

In an intelligent, connected and higher-evolutionary world, we need a third option beyond fight or flight, and that is thoughtfulness: a pause to think. Reflex is fine sometimes, and very useful in catching balls and avoiding deer crossing the road late at night, but we should always be capable of using our higher-evolutionary capabilities, namely those of meditation and/or intelligent, rational thought. Getting the balance right is crucial – between meditation and rational thought – and we must always beware hubris and arrogance.

A further debate within the spectrum of evolution, adaptation and learning is whether artificial intelligence has developed to such a level that we have already ceded control of our lives and life on planet Earth to the algorithmic formulas. Many global systems operate on semi-automatic, including

3 John Carey (ed.), *The Faber Book of Utopias* (London: Faber & Faber, 1999).

many financial transactions and communications technologies. For some, the question is whether we already have machines capable of mimicking human intelligence, and whether these machines are already in control. For others, the future for humankind as thinking beings may lie in becoming thinking, intelligent computers – as our planet becomes uninhabitable.

This apparent dichotomy may be a diversion from the real issue. Humans are subject to their environmental and evolutionary traits, many of which are now manufactured by the consumer mode of capitalism which plays on our innate desires.

A walk in the country or the bush will re-establish our evolutionary links to the land and Earth. The colours blue, green and red and the elements – water, earth, fire, rain and the sea – will always hold some sway on how we are minute by minute. If we can embrace the meditative and have confidence in a sense of not-knowing and awe, we will always have time to be thoughtful and rational in equal measure. So the major issue of our time may be distraction and seduction by forces designed by the powerful to lead us astray – whether they be social media or consumerism.

I also began this book by saying that I was no longer a miserablist. I have a positive outlook on humanity's future, even if it paradoxically means its demise. In the last century, while population has multiplied exponentially and may be out of control, most people have been lifted out of grinding poverty and most people now live in some sort of representative, semi-accountability state. This is not just because of capitalism, although it is clear that trade and the flow of knowledge have been enormous liberators, but also because of technological developments and social movements. The power of efficiency in mechanisation and the role of collectivism have been as important as the creation of so-called free markets. Indeed, the three issues – marketisation, collectivism and technology – are entwined components in political economy. The secret of the good society is to be found in the balance between different components.

The new international political economy

Earlier I said that globality is the dominant idea of the twenty-first century: knowing that we share one planet, that we are interconnected and interdependent are not only how the world is but also crucial for the survival of life on Earth. I argued for rebalancing science and awe so that we can have scientific and technological progress alongside time to think and time for thoughtfulness – what many would call mindfulness. Between the quick and the dead there should also be aimlessness, because it is in that space that creativity, love and sharing are best nurtured. I also pointed out the obvious: that an interconnected and interdependent world with a sense of its own survival needs different governance procedures and management skills. I said that this requires a rebalancing of yin and yang away from the masculine rapaciousness, competition, hunting and aggression that has characterised colonialism and industrial capitalism and towards more feminine virtues of sharing, nurturing, communication and gathering. But we should not lose sight of humans as creative problem solvers who require space and time to think, to be idiosyncratic, and to roam. In light of these issues, the obvious conclusion is that our institutions are no longer suited to the evolution, adaptation and learning that is now necessary to develop and survive on Earth. Neither are they in keeping with current technologies and knowledge developments.

So, in a sense, this last and fifth part of the book needs say no more than has already been said, But there are a few clarifications and additions to make concerning the nature of the nascent, ineluctable and necessary transitions now under way in social micro and macro systems.

Issues in the twenty-first century

In thinking about the evolution of global and local governance and the possibility of democracy, there is a strong need to be innovative and not hidebound by possible out-of-date ideas about meaning and practice. If we take a few of the fundamentals – such as human rights, the rule of law, the right to free association, and fundamental economic and political rights such as clean water, security, freedom of information and lack of discrimination based on gender, ethnicity, ability, sexuality or age – then there is much to be applauded so far and much to be built on, and much work still to do. But it's not a continuum, and the idea that the road is the same for all is spurious and misleading, for history dictates and each to her own.

There is a continuous media barrage about how bad things are and how full of evil the world is: it isn't, and we must resist the business and social media urge to shock and sell. That we can now see everything and at the same time know what our 'friends' had for breakfast is one of the shocks of this century. As Kenneth Gergen said in *The Saturated Self*, quoted earlier, how can we cope with this mental saturation? 'Am I bovvered?' Am I interested – how can I cope?

It is clear that from the evidence supplied from many sources, and previously cited from Piketty, Graeber and others, that on a global basis the wealth gap is increasing. The mid twentieth century saw an optimal phase where income distribution was most equal, when the highest percentage of people across many economies were in receipt of welfare and health benefits and when employment was as a full as it has ever been – just prior to the computerisation of labour and the introduction of the financialisation of everything.

The definition of the good society: full employment or usefulness; full health and welfare safety nets; income distribution; social mobility; educational entitlement; democratic political rights; relative peacefulness; and some meaningfulness in life, became a reality for many people across Europe and Scandinavia, in Canada, Australia and New Zealand, and, rapidly, in Japan between 1950 and 1980. This was a golden age, the long peace.

Today these economies offer many of the same opportunities but with the problems of unemployment, lower social mobility and the major issue of public debt to pay for the safety net and to prop up failing markets. But, as historian Tony Judt has pointed out, neither of the two superpowers, the USA and China, offer models that anyone else would want to copy. The USA offers a democratic deficit, unemployment, almost zero social mobility for the bottom 20%, 10% incarceration, the death penalty and a lack of gun control that in from Europe, Scandinavia, Japan and the Antipodes looks like civil war. China offers a total democratic deficit (albeit with extraordinary internet chatter on all matter of issues pertaining to democracy), as well as wealth disparity between the East and the West as great as anywhere in the world, significant social unrest (largely unreported inside and outside China), massive corruption, and difficulties maintaining the rule of law.[4] Both

4 See Judt and Snyder, *Thinking the Twentieth Century*.

countries maintain economic growth rates (using the traditional and outdated measure of economic growth), and both countries maintain the death penalty.

Interestingly, both the USA and China suffer from what has been called 'the inequality of the second machine age', where technology and cheap labour has created the 1/99% society. 1% own most of the wealth and 99% struggle to keep up: and these figures are as bad now as immediately prior to the stock market crash of 1929 and the hyperinflation of the 1930s that was one of the causes of the Second World War.[5] Incidentally, the UK also has wealth inequality figures similar to 1900. From the high point of 1968, Britain has depleted its social capital: social mobility is almost zero for the bottom 20%; housing prices are in crisis; and many public services are at risk of breaking down.

The movement of people from service to skills that took place as societies moved from agrarian economies to manufacturing and then on to highly skilled design and technology tracks is well documented by historian Eric Hobsbawm and others. But the trend towards poorly paid, menial tasks for the many while the very few make money from money is one of the most important and haunting issues for the twenty-first century and one of the drivers for the Occupy movement.

It is not just about the banks. The largest social media companies have found ways to make money on the back of selling empathy and at the same time pay almost zero tax to host governments who must light and police the streets and provide ambulances and hospital beds. Facebook, Twitter, Instagram and Google are as much beneficiaries of the Hayekian liberalisation of global markets as the banks – and we are all mugs.

---

5 See Brynjolfsson and McAfee, *The Second Machine Age.*

The ratios of creativity and skilled labour to wealth creation are staggering: Instagram was launched by four people and sold to Facebook for more than $1 billion within a few years. Facebook is run by 5,000 people and manages to pay minimal taxes to support the social structures we all rely on to make society work.

The irony is that companies like Google claim to love the idea of society (ironically, 'Don't be evil' is their motto), but trade on individualism and rational choice, while not supporting the idea of affective or built community at all. In the case of Google and Facebook, even their headquarters are outside town and separate from the communities where their workers live. The comparison with the gated communities of the East India Company and others in the nineteenth century is becoming more apparent.

The evidence, from both Danny Dorling's *Inequality and the 1%*[6] and Thomas Piketty's monumental study of *Capital in the Twenty-first Century*, is that it is significantly easier in a neoliberal capitalist economy to increase wealth if you already have wealth than to work your way up. For most people, investments are a matter of risking all their life savings – and earnings – and they have very few real choices. For those who already have wealth, Piketty concludes that the rich can take risks, and risk-taking often produces higher returns (and some losses), and most importantly, these people can pay for the best investment advice – and then make a choice. For the 1% linked to the deregulation of banking, it is easier to make money from gambling with money than investing in real goods and creating social wealth. As Adair Turner, Chairman of the UK's Financial Services Authority, has pointed out, banks being able to

---

6 Danny Dorling, *Inequality and the 1%* (London/New York: Verso Books, 2014; www.dannydorling.org/books/onepercent).

create credit was the primary cause of the 2008/9 crash. And since then this practice has not stopped and bankers are paying themselves vast sums from the credit they have created.[7]

For most people, simply selling their labour is as much as they can offer, and their investment opportunities are concerned with staying on the treadmill of mortgages, insurance, superannuation and pension funds with fingers crossed. The return for most of us for most of the twentieth century was about three or four per cent, whereas for those with established wealth the return has been as high as the best-performing economies: in other words, about seven to eight per cent.

If all you have to sell is your labour, then Marx was right: collect your fellows together and organise for a greater slice of the cake. Apart from unionisation, the lesson is very clear: public policy matters desperately when it comes to redistribution, predistribution, health and welfare safety nets, environmental protection and civil rights. Far from the state being obsolete, now is the time to rethink and re-empower the role of the local democratic unit, whether it be the street, the community, the city or the nation. There has to be a counter to the almighty momentum of the money market, the indiscriminate power of large, global corporations, and vagaries of the extremes within civil society.

The globalisation project was always economic, with politics riding on its back. In 1992, Francis Fukuyama tried to make us believe that neoliberal economics plus democracy equals the good life and the end of history. Similarly, in the seventeenth

7 Mira Tekelova, 'Adair Turner. The Clearest Explanation of the Cause of Financial Crisis', Positive Money, 7 November 2012; www.positivemoney.org/2012/11/adair-turner-the-clearest-explanation-of-the-cause-of-financial-crisis, accessed 2 December 2014.

century and for several hundred years afterwards, European powers and the USA strode into Africa and Asia and demanded that the locals trade or be defeated militarily. They were then exhorted to become traders, Christians and full-time workers in the economic system that had enslaved them – and in some cases they dramatically raised their standard of living. In a sense, then, ubiquity is also at the heart of globalisation: we should all be driving Toyotas, talking into iPhones, eating at Nando's, and flying Emirates. Every street corner should be the same.

In *Out of the Mountain: The Coming Age of the Urban Guerrilla*, David Kilcullen tells us that 'the future is crowded, coastal, urban and connected . . . We need to treat cities (not nation states) as the primary unit of analysis. We need to bring that analysis down to the city and the sub-city level, understanding communities and cities as systems in their own right' if we are to avoid urban guerrilla warfare.[8] Within this analysis is embedded the fact that the main growth in urban areas is in a country with no democratic rights: China.

The industrial revolution, starting in the UK with the enclosure of public land by private landlords, moved people from the land to the factories where work was plentiful but relentless and conforming of spirit and activity. As many have noted, the move from hunter-gathering and agriculture to industry enslaved most people while wealth was concentrated from the many to the few through the industrial working day. This is perfectly captured today by a description of the Quarry Bank

8 David Kilcullen, *Out of the Mountain: The Coming Age of the Urban Guerrilla* (Oxford, UK: Oxford University Press, 2013); see also David Kilcullen, 'Westgate Mall Attacks: Urban Areas are the Battleground of the 21st Century', *The Guardian*, 27 September 2013; www.theguardian.com/world/2013/sep/27/westgate-mall-attacks-al-qaida, accessed 5 December 2014.

working mill near Styal, preserved as an exhibit of nineteenth-century English industrial revolution: 'The new virtues that the workers were persuaded to adopt were those requisite for a material civilisation: regularity, punctuality, obedience, thrift, providence, sobriety, and industry.'

It is November 2013 and No. 17 serves me coffee in Shanghai; she's young but has no name – just a number on her lapel badge. This expensive service economy now holds in thrall the same number of affluent people as Europe or the United States of America. China is divided into three roughly equal economies: the affluent, the coming up fast, and the subsistent: 1.4 billion people in China in total, give or take a few hundred million. This wealth here, now, today, equals consumption and exploitation of the Earth's resources and the industrialisation of workers. Girl No. 17 doesn't work in a factory, as many, many millions do, making the parts for the world's iPhones and Lenovo gear. Within hours I'm weaving in and out of the traffic so quickly in this dreamland made real, it makes much of Europe and the US look very shabby, poor and run-down. This is globalisation writ large. It is a world of ubiquitous brands: the marketisation of life; while it grows, it works – but only while it grows. If the Chinese Communist Party can hold it together, I have no doubt that this economy will dominate all others this century.

In 2010 I was asked to inspect, in Shenzhen, China, a vast factory complex that makes printers and other electronic machines for Fuji Xerox and most of the brands that are seen around the world. They are all made on the same product lines with the same components. It is the branding, pricing and marketing that makes the difference. One of the rival factories, Foxconn, which makes components for Apple, had seen a large number of suicides by the young, migrant, formerly village-based, labour force.[9] Fuji Xerox did not want the same tragedy and opprobrium to hit them. I was asked to make an assessment. I chose my words carefully and I said that 'as far as I can see, from what I have been able to learn, this factory [the Fuji Xerox] factory is doing what it can, given that it is a manufacturing facility, to educate its workforce and to maintain health and safety regimes'.

One irony was that, in order to ensure that the Japanese-run factory had workers who would maintain the virtues that were extolled in the nineteenth-century Styal Mill of 'regularity, punctuality, obedience, thrift, providence, sobriety and industry', the company provided education in 'citizenship' – in a country with no tradition of democracy or engaged citizenship other than obedience to central rule.

It is projected that 'China will remain the main force driving global urbanisation over the next 20 years and the number of urban residents in China will increase by 268m over the period from 2010 to 2030, representing around one-fifth of global urban population growth over that period'.[10]

The issues of redefining the nation-state and moves towards smaller, more complex units of accountability such as the city and making more amorphous institutions such as large, global

9 See www.foxconn.com for information on the company; and for discussions on the various workplace ethics issues for this company, see Charles Duhigg and David Barboza, 'In China, Human Costs are Built into an iPad', *New York Times*, 25 January 2012; www.nytimes.com/2012/01/26/business/ieconomy-apples-ipad-and-the-human-costs-for-workers-in-china.html?pagewanted=all&_r=0, accessed 2 December 2014.

10 Economist Intelligence Unit, 'China's Urban Dreams, and the Regional Reality' (London: Economist Intelligence Unit, 2014; www.eiu.com/public/topical_report.aspx?campaignid=ChinaUrban Dreams, accessed 5 December 2014).

corporations more accountable require significant creativity, innovation and movement on the part of the very institutions that are threatened: the nation-states. It may be, as has happened before, that history overtakes on the outside and bypasses the nation-state. Or it may be that we are seeing a new hybrid: the corporation and the local community working together with civil society. We have seen this trisector arrangement repeatedly over the last twenty years delivering soft governance, but there are few examples of corporations really stepping up and delivering meaningful global public goods over the long term.

Which brings us to the issue of liberalism and neoliberalism. Samuel Huntington famously wrote of the clash of fundamentalisms between Christianity and Islam.[11] The real clash of fundamentalisms are those that have been outlined in this book, particularly between neoliberal economics and the planet, but they are fewer clashes of fundamentalism and more questions of rebalancing. The world has become too extreme. In other words, what is needed is an understanding of complex interactions and connections involving systems, and systems within systems. Overriding them all is the issue of harmony and balance. Through an outdated model of industrial capitalism we have too much yang and it needs rebalancing with the yin – men and the masculine need to move aside and let the gentle (who should 'inherit the Earth') and the feminine cooperator come inside. Too much yang is inherent in neoliberal economics, so market fundamentalism must be balanced with the long-term social good. And knowledge through natural philosophy and science needs to shine alongside scepticism and falsifiability. Deism has a place but only as an accompaniment to openness,

---

11 Samuel Huntington, *The Clash of Civilisations and the Remaking of World Order* (New York: Simon & Schuster, 1997).

wonder, awe and accountability – there should be no place for the mental glue of fundamentalism in any shape or form.

In the twenty-first-century good society – maintained at a local and a global level – people should be capable and independent and able to chart their own course, and yet understand that freedom does not mean licence: individual freedom is reliant on collective freedom and responsibility. Markets must not dominate social life and determine the future of the planet. Market fundamentalism has been found wanting, and one of the key issues, both social and environmental, at the heart of thinking about the twenty-first century is remarrying, or rebalancing, politics and economics. The new political economics must adopt a sustainable development purview and understand that people need capabilities like education, healthcare and civil rights as well as cash in order to be free, independent and creative individuals. These things mean an understanding and a reiteration of community, and, more fundamentally, society. We are not selfish automatons: we are individuals in communities – both affective and effective but bound by our evolutionary and adaptive past.[12]

Stewart Brand, author of the 1968 *Whole Earth Catalog*, said in 2013, 'lots of people try and change human nature but it's a waste of time. You can't change human nature but you can change tools, you can change techniques' and that way 'you can change civilisation.'[13] And changing civilisation, whatever thoughts one might have about the struggle for individual versus collective rights, may now be about raised consciousness

12 For a useful discussion of these issues, see Jon Cruddas and Jonathan Rutherford, 'The Liberal Republic', *New Statesman*, 18 June, 2009; www.newstatesman.com/books/2009/06/social-liberalism-reeves, accessed 2 December 2014.
13 Quoted in Cadwallader, 'Hippy, Radical, Genius, Visionary'.

(which may paradoxically come about through the integration of our brains and computers).

To counter this line of argument – that the solution to problems comes through technology – we must remind ourselves of Susan Greenfield's warning about the damage to our minds being wrought by social media.[14] Greenfield is a British scientist, writer, broadcaster and member of the House of Lords specialising in the physiology of the brain. Her research includes the impact of twenty-first-century technologies and how the brain 'generates' consciousness. In a similar vein, moral philosopher Jonathan Glover, referenced earlier, calls for a better understanding of how we think: for a greater emphasis on psychology.

> To avoid further disasters, we need political restraints on a world scale. But politics is not the whole story. We have experienced the results of technology in the service of the destructive side of human psychology. Something needs to be done about this fatal combination. The means for expressing cruelty and carrying out mass killing have been fully developed. It is too late to stop the technology. It is the psychology that we should now turn.[15]

On being human

Globality and Earth awareness are the dominant concepts of the twentieth and twenty-first centuries; in this context, the

14 www.susangreenfield.com, accessed 2 December 2014.
15 Glover, *Humanity*: 414.

two world wars gave us a sense, in a way that was not possible in previous centuries, of the one integrated place in which we physically live. World Wars I and II are not only turning points in understanding man's inhumanity to man but also in understanding of the idea of shared space and our place within it, and on it. Now that this sense is compounded by our growing understanding of Earth systems science, and particularly climate change science, the question 'What does it mean to be human now that we know what we know?' is both qualitatively and quantitatively different in this century compared to all previous attempts to address all aspects of the question.

Rachel Carson is revered as one of the founders of the modern environmental activist movement but she was as much a corporate responsibility writer and thinker. She was a thoughtful scientist, who, like Darwin and Lovelock, derived her ideas from sound enquiry and following the information wherever it led. Her toxicology work led her to analyse chemical repositories in birds and nature and then to ask questions about how they got there. Her research on high levels of dangerous toxic pesticides in birds led to two philosophical conclusions: that we have too much specialisation, thereby failing to make connections between different bodies of knowledge and to factor connectedness into policy decision-making; and that putting extreme technology in the hands of sales and business people produces sales without responsibility and economic growth without intelligent understanding or accountability.

Carson's incisiveness was matched by her sense of wonder and she wrote on awe as much as on science:

> The human race is challenged more than ever
> before to demonstrate our mastery, not over nature
> but of ourselves ... Only within the moment of
> time represented by the present century has one

species – man – acquired significant power to alter
the nature of the world.[16]

We need to stand back and look at ourselves from afar and
see ourselves for the first time, knowing that what we are seeing is but the latest view and there will be others if we keep an
open mind. Of course, science demands that we keep a constant open mind, or, as has often been quoted, 'the price of
freedom is eternal vigilance'. Science, like the ongoing discussions about sustainability, is a constant conversation with and
between ourselves concerning how we live, and how we live
on Earth. The author Julian Barnes writes in *Levels of Life*
that French balloonist Nadar's photos from above Paris were
one such moment of enlightenment for never before had people
seen their streets, houses and washing lines from above, looking down.

Similarly, the first images from space of Earth were transformative. When Neil Armstrong stepped on to the surface of
the Earth's Moon on 21st July 1969 at 02.56 GMT, before
his companion Buzz Aldrin could step down, he took movies
and stills of the new frontier – in case they had to depart in
haste. These images, combined with images taken from other
spacecraft outside the Earth's atmosphere before and after this
Moon landing, have changed the way humanity sees its spaceship, as Barbara Ward called Earth.[17] Seeing planethome for
the first time happened only yesterday and we have not come
to terms with it; but it was a life- and game-changing moment
for sentient beings. Now we could see the blue, delicate, fragile
place in space floating, floating among the stars. We are only
just beginning to appreciate where we are in the universe, no

16 Carson, *Silent Spring*: 23.
17 Ward, *Spaceship Earth*.

longer the centre of it but one small speck, ourselves as individuals just a smaller pinprick on the surface of a hot cosmic body.

In an age of science and highly developed technology, where demands for songs, images and information can be satisfied instantaneously, what seems to be needed most is open-mindedness while we try to come to terms for the first time with the reality of what, from different perspectives, Copernicus called heliocentrism and Lovelock calls Gaia theory. It is only two generations since we first looked back at ourselves through photographs taken of Earth and wondered at our vulnerability as a species, seeing the infinity of the universe, and our small home within it.

Isaac Newton, for all his mechanical mistakes, said that the development of microscopy produced the revelation for him that the more you looked at the detail of nature the more intricate and beautiful it became, but if you looked in detail at human inventions, such as an apparently sharp knife, they looked less perfect and less beautiful.

My first cystoscopy at the age of 59 was a similar revelation and not to be forgotten or amnesia'd because of its mission to check for signs of mortality. My surgeon, Ben, asked if I wanted to see on the screen as he progressed; and then we were on the journey down my penis, through the sphincter and past the prostate and into my bladder. Just as it must have been uncomfortable for the Moon landing men bundled up tight in their capsule, so the pain of entry into my innards past my sphincter was easily overcome by the beauty and momentousness of the vision of the inside of my body. Air bubbles, veins, pink, a scar from a previous nephrectomy, and all the time a running commentary: 'the Eagle has landed' or 'we're in and it's looking good with no sign of tumours, cancers or anything untoward'.

Similarly, on the Moon no diseases were found that might limit future landings. I was hooked, and still am, having never seen inside my own body before. For it is this body that carries around this head that pretends to write these words now, and the absolute wonder of it all is overwhelming. And yet, just as looking at the Earth from the Moon does not help us understand how the world works, so too looking inside my bladder doesn't explain how my urology functions; but in both cases the awe that is inspired allows us to meditate on something other than dispassionate knowledge.

Who does not want to spend a moment thinking about the fact that the stuff the astronauts saw as they gazed out across the universe is no different from the material I saw inside my body. Dust to dust, ashes to ashes. Science and enlightenment have always challenged nostrums and that is the story of Copernicus, Galileo, Darwin and Wallace, Carson, and lately Lovelock. In their time, their bravery as quiet leaders was seen at best as eccentricity and by others as madness.

The distance back from now to Socrates and Plato is just 98 generations. Writing, agriculture and cities is some 380 generations old and many would argue that the formation of our very humanness in the Pleistocene Age happened some 80,000 generations ago. We are now in the Anthropocene, which started at the beginning of the industrial revolution in the eighteenth century – about ten generations ago.

According to Denis Dutton, we retain landscape memories of where we came from, whoever we are, wherever we are, which comprise savannah with a low grassy area, interspersed with coppices or trees leading to water and a view of the horizon with some evidence of animal or bird life and a variety of greenery and fruiting plants.[18]

And so in times of difficulty we might turn to the joker and the poet. Perhaps we should turn to art for the truth, as science only shows us mystery and uncertainty and business makes the world stand on its head while our leaders lead us a merry dance on a pin. But 'music makes time stand still', and 'the novel tells the truth' – as conductor Colin Davis and novelist Julian Barnes have said, respectively.

How to see the world:
systems thinking and neuroplasticity

In 2012, Gro Harlem Brundtland said that for the first time humans know what they have done and know what they must do in order to adapt to climate change and other life-threatening issues.

In *The Story of the Human Body*, Daniel Lieberman writes: 'Our bodies are a hodge-podge of adaptation that accrued over a very long time and complex history . . . Now we're in this bizarre situation that for the first time in billions of years of evolution we have an organism that is not energy limited any more.'[19]

And it's a struggle, literally and metaphorically, because nature is too fecund and productive for all new life to survive

18 Denis Dutton, *The Art Instinct: Beauty, Pleasure, and Human Evolution* (Oxford, UK: Oxford University Press, 2009).

19 Daniel Lieberman *The Story of the Human Body: Evolution, Health and Disease* (London: Allen Lane, 2013), quoted in *The Observer*, 22 September 2013: The New Review, 23.

– and Charles Darwin never used the phrase 'the survival of the fittest'. This was a paraphrase by a journalist at the time of the publication of *On the Origin of Species*. What Darwin did say – that those most equipped to adapt have the best chance – is still pertinent today when discussing evolution, adaptation – and learning – because it is through rapid learning now that we may, as a species, find a way to change our current model of development from neoliberal economics to something more Earth- and people-centric. As with most of the shibbolethic writers of our age – Adam Smith and Karl Marx included – most need to be re-read to find out what they really said.

Not only that, but we are on the cusp, or in the midst, of changing our minds, according to Susan Greenfield: 'While we debate how to tackle the possibility of being doomed through climate change, we might be running as great a risk of a different peril: mind change – the prospect of cyber technologies changing the way we think and feel. The human brain is exquisitely sensitive to whatever environment it is placed in: this is its "neuroplasticity".'[20]

Every age claims to be new, but in the last century technology has left most people less able to review progress than in previous epochs. The two world wars in the first half of the twentieth century told us how technology could do its dirtiest and how we had become god – we could destroy ourselves. No longer is time glacial but seems to move at the speed of light. Arnold Toynbee in his 1970s monumental overview of history wrote that 'history is being made so fast . . . we don't have enough time to rethink the past and theories' and this is

---

20 Susan Greenfield, 'Are we all doomed?', *New Statesman*, 6 June 2011; https://www.newstatesman.com/society/2011/06/climate-change-doomed-brain, accessed 3 December 2014.

THINKING THE TWENTY-FIRST CENTURY

particularly true today as consumerism continuously encourages us to abandon yesterday for tomorrow.[21]

The history of life on Earth has been a history of interaction between living things and their surroundings. Carson talked about 'the rapidity and the speed with which new situations are created follow the impetuous and heedless pace of man rather than the deliberate pace of nature',[22] and Fritjof Capra said he shifted his research interests from 'physics to the life sciences to develop a conceptual framework that integrates four dimensions of life: the biological, the cognitive, the social, and the ecological'.[23]

Similarly, James Lovelock sees life in thinking systems – and his Gaia theory sees Earth as a single, self-regulating entity in which the organic and inorganic interact to sustain life. In 2014, at the age of 91, he said:

> I want to keep fighting the battle because the academics just won't buy it, whereas most other people have . . . It's political . . . You can't run a university unless it's divided into subjects. If you try and teach the whole lot, it becomes a complete mess and the vice-chancellor goes mad, so they have to divide it up. But if you divide it up, you can't understand it . . . The universities have reached a point similar to the monasteries in the middle ages where the

21 Toynbee, *A Study of History*: 13.
22 Carson, *Silent Spring*: 24.
23 Fritjof Capra, *The Web of Life: A New Scientific Understanding of Living Systems* (New York: Anchor Books, 1996); *The Hidden Connections: A Science for Sustainable Living* (London: HarperCollins, 2002); *The Systems View of Life: A Unifying Vision* (Cambridge, UK: Cambridge University Press, 2014).

monks counted the number of angels that could stand on the head of a needle.[24]

If Charles Darwin and James Lovelock have in common their transdisciplinarity and accessible writing, Rachel Carson has these qualities in spades. Rachel Carson stood down from her job as a toxicologist to write the book for which she is best known and in death much lauded: *Silent Spring*. Carson was inspired by children's authors like Beatrix Potter, creator of *Peter Rabbit, Jemima Puddleduck* and *Timmy Tiptoes*, and Kenneth Grahame, author of *The Wind in the Willows*, both of whom were also scientific observers and recorders of nature. In Potter's case, her mycological studies were a real inspiration to Carson, and her determination as a woman in a man's world also proved to be sustaining to Carson when she published counter-culture accounts of the relationship between human development and nature.

Published in 1962, Carson's work was rubbished by those whom she had attacked, namely pesticide and chemical manufacturers, but also she suffered misogynistic attacks from men who were confounded by a woman scientist with such authority who had caught the world's attention. Some things never change, as Professor Susan Greenfield will attest.

24 Stephen Moss, 'James Lovelock: "Instead of robots taking over the world, what if we join with them?" ', *The Guardian: G2*, 30 March 2014; www.theguardian.com/environment/2014/mar/30/james-lovelock-robots-taking-over-world, accessed 3 December 2014.

Quiet leadership

Leadership, when found in individuals, is an issue of deviancy. Most people are followers not leaders, and most leadership is found in social movements rather than heroic or charismatic individuals.

Management literature and airport bookstalls are awash with books on leadership – thirty-nine steps, five easy pieces, ten blue bottles, a dozen eggs in the basket, one way straight to heaven and other catchy but daft titles. They sell because we all seek quick solutions, because one person's rise must be a model for everyone else, and because in the business and management literature success equals money. Points mean prizes.

But very few of these 'guru'-led books combine good and evil, success and failure, immorality and morality, business and politics. Some of the few business and management books in the last decade that have focused on leadership (individual) for the good society and sustainability are interesting for pointing out that we are often led by the most appallingly self-centred and evil people who have no interest in public good or the fate of the Earth. And, of course, often the best individual leaders arrive at the right moment and become symbolic of a movement.

For example, two of the best twentieth-century British political leaders, Winston Churchill and Clement Attlee, were so different in character, demeanour and performance, and had different political agendas. Churchill, a brilliant orator and writer with a first-class mind was a one-nation conservative who knew only the rigidity of British class system, while Attlee was a quiet, social reformer *par excellence* who introduced the world's first *national* free-at-the-point-of-delivery-to-all health system to the UK along with universal secondary education.

Out of the war that Churchill had 'won', Attlee made the peace and built the society that has prospered for the last seventy years. While Churchill's leadership style is much lauded, and his speechmaking much copied (Tony Blair's and Barack Obama's oratory is full of examples of Churchillian short clipped sentences, with a pause), few books on leadership hold up Clement Attlee's quiet, soft-spoken manner as an example. But in a five-year term as Prime Minister he got things done, leading Britain out of the literal and metaphorical rubble of the Second World War, having won a landslide victory over Churchill in 1945. He was Labour Party leader for twenty years.

The one other British political leader who ought to be remembered is Harold Wilson, who, apart from leading the most equal Britain there has ever been, persistently and quietly refused to be bullied by the US into getting involved in the disastrous Vietnam War. His other legacy is the establishment of the Open University, then in the 1960s a miracle, and now replicated online extensively. Similarly, in the US the passionate, morality-driven US President Jimmy Carter only served one term but his post-presidential work as a peacemaker has been substantial, perhaps more useful than his time in office.

Niccolò Machiavelli is much quoted, as he is a distant figure and seen as strategic, as is Sun Tzu, but more modern leaders are not studied as much they might be as examples of ethical leadership. Where are the airport books to guide ethical leadership on the subject of these men: Adolf Hitler, Josef Stalin, Mao Tse-tung and Pol Pot – and all their many acolytes, men and women?

All leaders serve a cause: theirs or society's. The issues of evil and madness are important when discussing leadership; as Shakespeare had Malvolio say in *Twelfth Night*: 'Some are born great, some achieve greatness, and some have greatness thrust upon them.' Those that have 'greatness thrust upon them' we can call quiet leaders. Shakespeare was a 'quiet leader' who achieved greatness not by leading from the front but by hard work, aptitude and example – the example being his written and acting work. Also quiet leaders are Thomas Paine, Rachel Carson, Charles Darwin and James Lovelock, who all led from the rear by changing minds through intelligent thought, diligent research and the ability to put pen to paper (fingers to keys). Their influence only become apparent when their thoughts form the core values of a social movement that proselytises to the world.

The political leaders from the twentieth century listed previously – Adolf Hitler, Josef Stalin, Mao Tse-tung and Pol Pot – were men of their time. There have been many attempts to rationalise the evil that these men are responsible for – 'the evil that men do lives after them' – and I have no desire to absolve them from evil – but two issues remain. First, the concept of evil is elusive: we know it when we see it, but we often collude with its origins and then disown it. Second, these men did not act alone – they had both acolytes and followers.

At Nelson Mandela's funeral in 2013 a number of post-independence, post-colonial leaders spoke, including Hailemariam Desalegn, Prime Minister of Ethiopia, Jakaya Kikwete, President of Tanzania, and Joyce Banda, President of Malawi. She said Mandela had inspired her to become the first female president in southern Africa: 'Leadership,' she said, 'is about falling in love with the people you serve and about the people falling in love with you.'

Followership is as important as leadership; indeed, they are two sides of the same coin. Good and evil are social constructs, and what we now see as evil (for instance, mass extermination and genocide) has been commonplace in human history. How else, for instance, would Europeans have gained their empires, and the Mongols crossed all of Asia and into Europe?

Some of those who survived the German concentration camps of WWII have written about that evil, notably Bruno Bettelheim, Viktor Frankl and Primo Levi. In *The Zone of Interest* the novelist Martin Amis has commented on the corrosive effect of trying to understand evil that is beyond understanding. As he says, echoing Levi, to try to explain is to try to contain, to rationalise and therefore banish.[25] If we can measure it, we can manage it, the thought goes. To repeat: followership is as important as leadership; indeed, they are two sides of the same coin.

It is often commented that those who rise to power must be different from other people. Power means managing the slings and arrows of outrageous fortune and managing responsibilities that most people do not want. Leaders should be respected, but most of all they should be accountable. Lord Acton's maxim that 'Power tends to corrupt, and absolute power corrupts absolutely. Great men are almost always bad men' should always be borne in mind; the US constitutional founders knew this was so when they limited presidents to two terms – a maximum of eight years. That provision would have helped many other countries and would have been very helpful for many companies too. It's an issue of constitutional and corporate governance.

Social dysfunctionality is a characteristic of academics (and politicians – and all leaders?) and many professional positions. Kevin Dutton, among others, has derived a list of the most psychopathic jobs – he may mean sociopathic, but these two terms

25 Martin Amis, *The Zone of Interest* (London: Jonathan Cape, 2014); see also 'Here there is no why', *Financial Times*, 23–24 August 2014: 7.

seem to be used differently in the USA and elsewhere. Dutton's ranking in *The Wisdom of Psychopaths* does not specifically include politicians and academics, who are absent from the top ten, it would appear, although many academics and politicians hold, or have held, these positions. A psychopath is described as an antisocial person, whose personality disorders include deceitfulness. They have a high self-worth, a strong focus on the positive, and are reward-driven.[26]

Dutton's top 10 psychopathic jobs

1. CEO
2. Lawyer
3. Media (TV/radio)
4. Salesperson
5. Surgeon
6. Journalist
7. Police officer
8. Cleric
9. Chef
10. Civil servant

This is one reason why leadership studies should always be accompanied by studies of followership.

There is a distinction to be drawn between leaders and changemakers, wayfinders or sensemakers. Leaders may be all of these but they are more often focused on a single aim, often themselves. Leaders who combine the qualities of changemaking, wayfinding or sensemaking are rare. But I also want to raise another issue. In order to make the changes that are now necessary (and may be nascent and ineluctable), I want to argue that good leadership involves adaptation, which comes

26 Kevin Dutton, *The Wisdom of Psychopaths: Lessons in Life from Saints, Spies and Serial Killers* (London: Heinemann, 2012).

through learning. Open learning involves a polymath approach to knowledge. All of the quiet leaders noted in this book are polymaths, and perhaps it's true that geniuses are also polymaths (or, rather, polymaths are geniuses?).

It has often been noted that a person recognised as the inventor of such-and-such is actually a representative of his or her age and tends to be one of a crowd on the same creative track. So Watt and Stephenson are the men we remember, but they weren't the only people working on the steam engine and the steam train respectively. It is often forgotten that the Romans had steam engines for use in children's toys but had never thought of using them for locomotion. Similarly, the Chinese used gunpowder for millennia for fireworks, not for warfare. That took a Swede, Alfred Nobel, of the Peace Prize, to turn it to 'good' use in killing people. And it took an Austrian farmer, Friedrich Hayek, to make us afraid of cities, urbanisation and planning because he saw the complex interactions and thinking that is natural to areas of dense population as breeding places for Marxism and Communism – and planning. Therefore, he hated public policy planning.

This idea – that representatives of innovations and ideas are our heroic reminders – is exemplified in most Western art galleries: their international collections all have a similar representative sample of Monet, Picasso, Hockney, Moore, Pollock and others. This highlights the problem we have today at a moment of great change – a transitional moment: thinking using our siloed mentality and exclusive debates and thereby dismissing the opportunities of polymathic thinking. Just as it took two world wars and their concomitant seismic shifts on social mobility and poverty awareness for Clement Attlee and the Labour Party to introduce the world's first national health service in the UK, so it may take similarly cataclysmic events to produce the necessary shifts in paradigmatic thinking.

We now see learning to live as one diverse people on planet Earth to be a desirable aim, a social good. We can focus on how this end might be achieved, or rescued from the past. How can we recover our innocence and find a future that allows for perpetuity and some sense of sustainability – albeit illusory, given our individual mortality? A number of writers and activists, who would call themselves social entrepreneurs, green activists and intellectual shamans, through in-depth research have quantified what is necessary.

Sandra Waddock in her survey of 'difference makers' noted that these leaders (of different ways of being, doing and thinking) were outsiders, not driven by money or power but with a focus on a progressive view of the public good.[27] All her 23 difference makers (in social activism, thought leadership or business) knew how to mobilise social movements and were often engaged in the responsible assurance of, and accountability in, large and powerful institutions. They operated from within the system by creating change at the edge. She suggested they were modest by nature (she may have misunderstood non-US self-effacement): some of these people may be dogged and determined but not necessarily modest. My experience of working with them is that they, like myself, have some of the qualities of Dutton's psychopaths (sociopaths): obsession and reward focus – with the reward being social rather than personal wealth or power.

John Elkington's successful social entrepreneurs are not constrained by the status quo; they are innovative, resourceful and

27 Sandra Waddock, *The Difference Makers: How Social and Institutional Entrepreneurs Created the Corporate Responsibility Movement* (Sheffield, UK: Greenleaf Publishing, 2008).

opportunistic with a focus on social value creation. They jump early and have a strong belief in the possibility because they are risk takers. Having taken the risk – in favour of social change through entrepreneurship – they closely monitor the impact noting particularly the cross-fertilisation into other sectors. These people, like Waddock's difference makers, are impatient and hate bureaucracies.[28] I identify with these people who cannot understand everyone else's institutional inertia and their cosying up to the nest rather than trying to build a better, more resilient nest away from the impending flood. Can't they see their own shadow on the wall, or am I being too Hegelian? It's OK to be 'good enough', as Bruno Bettelheim would have us be (when he was talking about parenting), but some of us are never satisfied.

Sara Parkin's thinking builds on the two frameworks outlined here. In *The Positive Deviant* she says that this sort of person 'does the right thing for sustainability, despite being surrounded by the wrong institutional structures, the wrong structures and stubbornly uncooperative people'. Their four habits of thought resonate with Waddock's and Elkington's analyses. They are resilient and bounce back and they build social capital through relationships with like-minded, sustainability-literate people who understand the complexity of this subject area. Because this work is difficult and frustrating – three steps forward, two, three or four steps back – they are able to pause and reflect and then decide and act. They have reverence for life, and for life on Earth, and are happy to be in awe, to not be in charge. As she says, we are less likely to hurt others when we love and revere ourselves, others and our environment. The

28 John Elkington and Pamela Hartigan, *The Power of Unreasonable People: How Social Entrepreneurs Create Markets That Change the World* (Boston, MA: Harvard Business Press, 2008).

lessons from Parkin's book and her life work as a dedicated environmental and social activist are to have more respect for nature, to be in awe not in charge, and to adapt or die.[29]

We could add to this that it is very important to learn from history; to teach Earth systems science; to lower population; to adapt the current model of rapacious capitalism and develop sustainable enterprise economies; to tread lightly on planet Earth; and to love and respect the Earth as you love your children.

I would also want to add that, to make sense of this noisy world, we need to actively plan for quiet contemplation, for it is in the silence that we will understand wisdom.

Also, we need space for creativity and mistake-making; as Grayson Perry, the award-winning artist, says: 'The minute you try to be original you are probably going to fail because those things happen out of the corner of your eye, when you are striving for something else.'[30] Beatrix Potter's comment that her education was neglected, referenced earlier, isn't an argument against schooling but *for* education and the need to develop polymaths, or, as I argued earlier, to go back to the idea of natural philosophers – this is the future of education. How else will we produce Carsons, Lovelocks, Darwins, Goldings, Smiths or Marxes?

And, in ending, let me reference again the thoughts of the toxicologist, the reflective politician, the novelist and the artist. For theirs is a greater wisdom than can be wrought from any atomised academic paper.

29 Sara Parkin, *The Positive Deviant: Sustainability Leadership in a Perverse World* (London: Earthscan, 2010).

30 Turner Prize winner (2003) Grayson Perry, quoted in 'Weird Alleyways of Culture', *The Economist*, 1 January 2011; www.economist.com/node/21530941, accessed 3 December 2014.

Not a great deal has changed since Rachel Carson wrote in 1962 that 'this is an era of specialists, each of whom sees his own problem and is unaware of or intolerant of the larger frame into which it fits'.[31] 'It is also an era dominated by industry, in which the right to make a dollar at whatever cost is seldom challenged. When the public protests . . . It is fed little tranquillizing pills of half truths.'

Václav Havel, the first Czech Republic President, taking a summer break in 1992 in his presidency, wrote meditatively: 'I have become aware of how immensely difficult it is to be guided in practice by the principles and ideals in which I believe. But, I have not abandoned them in any way.'[32]

Ai Weiwei, designer of the 2008 Beijing Olympics and under house arrest in 2014 in Beijing, speaks similarly of the way art can transcend the obvious and reach beyond the material, thereby linking form, function and aspiration and so raising the spirit. In words to accompany his sculpture 'Iron Tree' in 2013, he said: 'Society allows artists to explore what we don't know in ways that are distinct from the approaches of science, religion and philosophy. As a result, art bears a unique responsibility in the search for truth.' Being Chinese, his words speak particularly to unethical government policies and issues of surveillance, transparency, communication and truth in real and virtual worlds.[33]

In a global world, in learning about its interdependencies we must not forget our evolutionary past; but we should accelerate the positive that is to be found in relating evolution to

---

31 Carson, *Silent Spring*: 29.
32 Havel, *Summer Meditations*: xiii.
33 Ai Weiwei quoted in an exhibition at Yorkshire Sculpture Park, UK, 27 October 2014, where, ironically, CCTV was in operation and no photography was allowed.

adaptation and learning – and we should do this fast. If the forces of inertia, conservatism, fear, institutional self-satisfaction and market failure hold us back from embracing and furthering the nascent changes outlined in this book, we will fail and this may be humankind's last century.

But, in bringing together the complex issues of globality, science, feminism, organisation, evolution, adaptation and learning, I hope this book adds a mite of wisdom to our collective consciousness. If it adds as much as I have learnt in its writing, it will have made considerable change. I am hopeful and smiling.

Bibliography

Adams, Tim (2014) 'Testosterone and high finance do not mix: So bring on the women', *The Observer*, 19 June 2011; www. theguardian.com/world/2011/jun/19/neuroeconomics-women-city-financial-crash, accessed 14 December 2014.

Ahmeed, Nafeez (2014) 'Nasa-Funded Study: Industrial Civilisation Headed for "Irreversible Collapse"?', *The Guardian*, 14 March 2014; www.theguardian.com/environment/earth-insight/2014/mar/14/nasa-civilisation-irreversible-collapse-study-scientists.

Aguilera, Pilar, and Ricardo Fredes (eds.) (2006) *Chile: The Other September 11. An Anthology of Reflections on the 1973 Coup* (Minneapolis, MN/Melbourne, VIC: Ocean Press).

Amis, Martin (2014a) *The Zone of Interest* (London: Jonathan Cape).

Amis, Martin (2014b) 'Here there is no why', *Financial Times*, 23–24 August 2014: 7.

Atwood, Margaret (1972) *Survival: A Thematic Guide to Canadian Literature* (Toronto: House of Anansi Press).

Atwood, Margaret (2014) 'Rachel Carson's *Silent Spring*, 50 years on', *The Guardian*, 7 December 2012; www.theguardian.com/books/2012/dec/07/why-rachel-carson-is-a-saint, accessed 1 December 2014.

Barber, Brad M., and Terrance Odean (2001) 'Boys Will Be Boys: Gender, Overconfidence, and Common Stock Investment', *Quarterly Journal of Economics* 116.1: 261-92.

Barnes, Julian (2012) *Through the Window: Seventeen Essays (and One Short Story)* (London: Vintage).

Bateson, Gregory (1972) *Steps to an Ecology of Mind: Collected Essays in Anthropology, Psychiatry, Evolution, and Epistemology* (Chicago: University of Chicago Press).

Blakemore, Colin (2001) 'Interview with James Lovelock', *The Observer*, 12 June 2011: 21.

Bowen, Jeremy (2014) 'Notebook', *New Statesman*, 7–13 March 2014: 22.

Brockes, Emma (2013) 'Julian Barnes: The Sense of Another Ending', *The Guardian*, 30 March 2013; www.theguardian.com/books/2013/mar/30/julian-barnes-sense-of-another-ending, accessed 1 December 2014.

Brundtland, Gro Harlem (2012) 'Earth Agonistes', *International Herald Tribune*, 19 June 2012: 8.

Brynjolfsson, Erik, and Andrew McAfee (2014) *The Second Machine Age: Work, Progress, and Prosperity in a Time of Brilliant Technologies* (New York/London: Norton).

Burke, Jason (2014) 'Rana Plaza: One Year On from the Bangladesh Factory Disaster', *The Guardian*, 19 April 2014; www.theguardian.com/world/2014/apr/19/rana-plaza-bangladesh-one-year-on, accessed 5 December 2014.

Cadwallader, Carole (2013) 'Hippy, Radical, Genius, Visionary . . . And the First Man in Cyberspace', *The Observer*, 5 May 2013: 8-11.

Cannadine, David (2013) *The Undivided Past: History Beyond Our Differences* (London: Allen Lane).

Capra, Fritjof (1982) *The Turning Point: Science, Society and the Rising Culture* (New York: Simon & Schuster).

Capra, Fritjof (1996) *The Web of Life: A New Scientific Understanding of Living Systems* (New York: Anchor Books).

Capra, Fritjof (2002) *The Hidden Connections: A Science for Sustainable Living* (London: HarperCollins).

Capra, Fritjof (2014) *The Systems View of Life: A Unifying Vision* (Cambridge, UK: Cambridge University Press).

Capra, Fritjof, and Pier Luigi Luisi (2014) *The Systems View of Life: A Unifying Vision* (Cambridge, UK: Cambridge University Press).

Carey, John (ed.) (1999) *The Faber Book of Utopias* (London: Faber & Faber).

Carey, John (2009) *William Golding: The Man who Wrote* Lord of the Flies (London: Penguin Modern Classics).

Carson, Rachel (1962) *Silent Spring* (Boston, MA: Houghton Mifflin).

Cassells, Richard (2013) 'The Devil is in the Synergy. The Exhibitions at MOSET: A Hypothetical Museum of Human Transitions', in Malcolm McIntosh (ed.), *The Necessary Transition: The Journey towards the Sustainable Enterprise Economy* (Sheffield, UK: Greenleaf Publishing): 51-79.

Cernan, Eugene (2002) 'This Much I Know', *Observer Magazine*, 16 June 2002: 6.

Chomsky, Noam (1993) *The Prosperous Few and the Restless Many* (Tucson, AZ: Odonian Press).

Chomsky, Noam (2011) *How The World Works* (Berkeley, CA: Soft Skull Press).

Cleave, Maureen (2005) 'The John Lennon I Knew', *The Telegraph*, 5 October 2005; www.telegraph.co.uk/culture/music/rockandjazzmusic/3646983/The-John-Lennon-I-knew.html, accessed 1 December 2014.

Colvin, Naomi, and Kai Wargalla (2011) What we're really doing at St Paul's', *The Guardian*, 23 October 2011; www.theguardian.com/commentisfree/2011/oct/23/way-forward-99-occupy-london, accessed 14 December 2014.

Costa, Ken (2011) 'Why the city should heed the discordant voices of St Paul's', *Financial Times*, 28 October 2011; on.ft.com/1GiozKT, accessed 5 March 2014.

Crouch, Colin (2011) *The Strange Non-death of Neoliberalism* (Cambridge, UK: Polity Press).

Cruddas, Jon, and Jonathan Rutherford (2014) 'The Liberal Republic', *New Statesman*, 18 June, 2009; www.newstatesman.com/books/2009/06/social-liberalism-reeves, accessed 2 December 2014.

Darwin, Charles (1859) *On Natural Selection* (excerpts from *On the Origin of Species*, ed. J.W. Burrow; Camberwell, VIC: Penguin Books, 2004).

Dawkins, Richard (1982) *The Extended Phenotype: The Long Reach of the Gene* (Oxford, UK: Oxford University Press).

Diamond, Bob (2011) 'Today Business Lecture 2011', BBC; news.bbc.co.uk/today/hi/today/newsid_9630000/9630673.stm, accessed 5 March 2014.

Diamond, Jared (2012) *The World until Yesterday: What Can We Learn from Traditional Societies?* (London: Allen Lane).

Dorling, Danny (2014) *Inequality and the 1%* (London/New York: Verso Books; www.dannydorling.org/books/onepercent).

Drucker, Peter F. (1946) *Concept of the Corporation* (Piscataway, NJ: Transaction Publishers, 1993).

Drucker, Peter F. (1973) *Management: Tasks, Responsibilities, Practices* (New York: HarperBusiness, 1993).

Drucker, Peter F. (1993) *Post-Capitalist Society* (New York: HarperBusiness).

Drucker, Peter F. (2001) *The Essential Drucker: The Best of Sixty Years of Peter Drucker's Essential Writings on Management* (New York: HarperCollins).

Dutton, Denis (2009) *The Art Instinct: Beauty, Pleasure, and Human Evolution* (Oxford, UK: Oxford University Press).

Dutton Kevin (2012) *The Wisdom of Psychopaths: Lessons in Life from Saints, Spies and Serial Killers* (London: Heinemann).

Duhigg, Charles, and David Barboza (2012) 'In China, Human Costs are Built into an iPad', *New York Times*, 25 January 2012; www.nytimes.com/2012/01/26/business/ieconomy-apples-ipad-and-the-human-costs-for-workers-in-china. html?pagewanted=all&_r=0, accessed 2 December 2014.

Economist (2011) 'Weird Alleyways of Culture', *The Economist*, 1 January 2011; www.economist.com/node/21530941, accessed 3 December 2014.

Economist Intelligence Unit (2014) 'China's Urban Dreams, and the Regional Reality' (London: Economist Intelligence Unit; www.eiu.com/public/topical_report.aspx?campaignid=China UrbanDreams, accessed 5 December 2014).

Edelman, 'Trust in Government Plunges to Historic Low: Business Trust Stabilizes, Creating Largest Gap Ever Between Trust in Government and Business', Edelman press release, 19 January 2014; www.edelman.com/news/trust-in-government-plunges-to-historic-low, accessed 19 February 2014.

Einstein, Albert (1979) *Autobiographical Notes* (Chicago: Open Court Publishing Company).

Elkington, John, and Pamela Hartigan (2008) *The Power of Unreasonable People: How Social Entrepreneurs Create Markets That Change the World* (Boston, MA: Harvard Business Press).

Foucault, Michel (2007) 'Key Concepts'; www.michel-foucault. com/concepts, accessed 5 December 2014.

Friedman, Milton (1970) 'The Social Responsibility of Business is to Increase its Profits', *New York Times Magazine*, 13 September 1970; www.umich.edu/~thecore/doc/Friedman.pdf).

Fukuyama, Francis (1992) *The End of History and The Last Man* (London: Penguin).

Fukuyama, Francis (2014) *Political Order and Political Decay: From the Industrial Revolution to the Globalization of Democracy* (New York: Farrar Straus Giroux).

Gergen, Kenneth J. (1991) *The Saturated Self: Dilemmas of Identity in Contemporary Life* (New York: Basic Books).

Glover, Jonathan (2001) *Humanity: A Moral History of the Twentieth Century* (New Haven, CT: Yale University Press).

Goldenberg, Suzanne (2012) 'Obama Scored Big with Single Women', *Guardian Weekly*, 16 November 2012: 4.

Golding, William (1954) *Lord of the Flies* (London: Faber & Faber).

Gray, John (2013) 'Man for All Seasons', *New Statesman*, 22–28 March 2013: 34.

Greene, Brian (2011) 'Are we all doomed?', *New Statesman*, 6 June 2011: 25.

Greenfield Susan (2011) 'Are we all doomed?', *New Statesman*, 6 June 2011; https://www.newstatesman.com/society/2011/06/climate-change-doomed-brain, accessed 3 December 2014.

Grin, John, Jan Rotmans and Johan Schot (2010) *Transitions to Sustainable Development: New Directions in the Study of Long Term Transformative Change* (New York/London: Routledge).

Hamilton, Clive (2010) *Requiem for a Species: Why We Resist the Truth about Climate Change* (London: Earthscan).

Harari, Yuval (2014) *Sapiens: A Brief History of Humankind* (London: Harvill Sekker).

Hardt, Michael, and Antonio Negri (2000) *Empire* (Cambridge, MA: Harvard University Press).

Havel, Václav (1992) *Summer Meditations* (London: Vintage Books).

Hayek, Friedrich (1944) *The Road to Serfdom* (London: Routledge).

Hemmer, Nicole (2012) 'It's the women wot won it: Democrat victory was not fluke', *The Conversation* (Australia), 8 November 2012.

Hepworth, Katherine (2012) 'Gillard's misogyny speech looks even better than it reads', *The Conversation* (Australia), 14 October 2012.

Hobsbawm, Eric (1962) *The Age of Revolution. Europe: 1789–1848* (London: Abacus).

Hobsbawm, Eric (1975) *The Age of Capital: 1848–1875* (London: Weidenfeld & Nicolson).

Huntington, Samuel (1997) *The Clash of Civilisations and the Remaking of World Order* (New York: Simon & Schuster).

Hutton, James (1788) *Theory of the Earth; or an Investigation of the Laws Observable in the Composition, Dissolution, and Restoration of Land upon the Globe* (Sioux Falls, SD: NuVision Publications, 2007).

Judd, Ron (2012) 'With a View from beyond the Moon: An Astronaut Talks Religion, Politics and Possibilities', *Seattle Times*, 7 December 2012.

Judt, Tony, with Timothy Snyder (2012) *Thinking the Twentieth Century* (London: Vintage).

Kahneman, Daniel (2011) *Thinking Fast and Slow* (London: Allen Lane).

Kay, John (2013) 'Circular Thinking: Models that offer universal descriptions of the world have led economists to repeat their mistakes', *RSA Journal* 4.

Kellner, Peter (2012) 'Thank Fox for that', *Prospect* (UK), December 2012.

Kilcullen, David (2013) *Out of the Mountain: The Coming Age of the Urban Guerrilla* (Oxford, UK: Oxford University Press).

Kilcullen David (2014) 'Westgate Mall Attacks: Urban Areas are the Battleground of the 21st Century', *The Guardian*, 27 September 2013; www.theguardian.com/world/2013/sep/27/westgate-mall-attacks-al-qaida, accessed 5 December 2014.

King, Martin Luther (1967) 'Beyond Vietnam', speech, Riverside Church, New York City, 4 April 1967; mlk-kpp01.stanford.edu/index.php/encyclopedia/encyclopedia/enc_beyond_vietnam_4_april_1967, accessed 28 November 2014.

Krauss, Lawrence M. (2012) *A Universe from Nothing: Why There Is Something Rather Than Nothing* (New York: Free Press).

Krznaric, Roman (2014) 'Is Australia losing its empathy?', *The Guardian*, 25 February 2014; www.theguardian.com/culture/australia-culture-blog/2014/feb/26/is-australia-losing-its-empathy, accessed 28 November 2014.

Lacey, Hester (2012) 'A Walk with the FT: The Golden Cap Route', *Financial Times*, 5 June 2012; www.ft.com/cms/s/2/ce351d3e-a473-11e1-a701-00144feabdc0.html, accessed 28 November 2014.

Lanchester, John (2010) *Whoops! Why Everyone Owes Everyone and No One Can Pay* (London: Allen Lane).

Lanchester, John (2014a) 'How to speak money – and why you need to learn', *The Telegraph*, 9 August 2014; www.telegraph.co.uk/culture/books/11022772/How-to-speak-money-and-why-you-need-to-learn, accessed 1 December 2014.

Lanchester, John (2014b) 'What's Your Position on Octopus?', *Financial Times*, 30–31 August 2014: 3.

Lanier, Jaron (2013) *Who Owns The Future?* (London: Allen Lane).

Lee, Chris (1994) 'The Feminisation of Management', *Training* 31.11: 25-31.

Lewis, Michael (2011a) *The Big Short: Inside the Doomsday Machine* (London: Penguin).

Lewis, Michael (2011b) *Boomerang: The Meltdown Tour* (London: Penguin).

Lieberman, Daniel (2013) *The Story of the Human Body: Evolution, Health and Disease* (London: Allen Lane).

Lucas, Clay (2012) 'Women most empowered in world but men still rule the roost on pay', *Sydney Morning Herald*, 17 October 2012; bit.ly/1zfxjkW, accessed 14 December 2014.

Marx, Karl (1852) *The Eighteenth Brumaire of Louis Bonaparte*, 1852; https://www.marxists.org/archive/marx/works/1852/18th-brumaire/ch01.htm, accessed 16 December 2014

Maturana, Humberto R., and Francisco Varela (1998) *The Tree of Knowledge: The Biological Roots of Human Understanding* (London/Boston, MA: Shambala).

Mayer, Colin (2013) *Firm Commitment: Why the corporation is failing us and how to restore trust in it* (Oxford, UK: Oxford University Press).

McIntosh, Malcolm (1986) *Japan Re-armed* (repr. edn; London: Bloomsbury, 2013).

McIntosh, Malcolm (2003) 'PlanetHome', in Rupesh A. Shah, David F. Murphy and Malcolm McIntosh (eds.), *Something To Believe In: Creating Trust and Hope in Organisations: Stories of Transparency, Accountability and Governance* (Sheffield, UK: Greenleaf Publishing): 24-29.

McIntosh, Malcolm (ed.) (2013) *The Necessary Transition: The Journey towards the Sustainable Enterprise Economy* (Sheffield, UK: Greenleaf Publishing).

McIntosh, Malcolm, and Sandra Waddock (2012) 'Learning from the Roundtables on the Sustainable Enterprise Economy: The United Nations Global Compact and the Next Ten Years', in Andreas Rasche and Georg Kell (eds.), *The United Nations Global Compact: Achievements, Trends and Opportunities* (Cambridge, UK: Cambridge University Press): 215-33.

McLaren, Malcolm (2008) 'This Much I Know', *Observer Magazine*, 16 November 2008: 10.

Meadows, Donella H. (2008) *Thinking in Systems: A Primer* (White River Junction, VT: Chelsea Green Publishing).

Mirowski, Philip (2013) *Never Let a Serious Crisis Go to Waste: How Neoliberalism Survived the Financial Meltdown* (London/New York: Verso Books).

Mishra, Pankaj (2012a) *From The Ruins of Empire: The Revolt against the West and the Remaking of Asia* (London: Penguin).

Mishra, Pankaj (2012b) 'A Righteous Nostalgia', *The Guardian*, 28 July 2012: Review, 2.

Moody-Stuart, Mark (2014) 'Business as a Vocation', *Journal of Corporate Citizenship* 55 (September 2014): 9-12.

Moss, Stephen (2014) 'James Lovelock: "Instead of robots taking over the world, what if we join with them?" ', *The Guardian*: G2, 30 March 2014; www.theguardian.com/environment/2014/mar/30/james-lovelock-robots-taking-over-world, accessed 3 December 2014.

Motesharrei, Safa, Jorge Rivas and Eugenia Kalnay (2014) 'Human and Nature Dynamics (HANDY): Modeling Inequality and Use of Resources in the Collapse or Sustainability of Societies', *Ecological Economics* 101 (May 2014): 90-102.

O'Rourke, P.J. (1998) *Eat the Rich: A Treatise on Economics* (London: Picador).

Paine, Thomas (1824) *The Theological Works of Thomas Paine* (London: R. Carlile).

Parkin, Sara (2010) *The Positive Deviant: Sustainability Leadership in a Perverse World* (London: Earthscan).

Pembroke, Michael (2013) *Arthur Phillip: Sailor, Mercenary, Governor, Spy* (Melbourne/London: Hardie Grant Books).

Peston, Robert (2012) *How Do We Fix This Mess? The Economic Price of Having it All, and the Route to Lasting Prosperity* (London: Hodder & Stoughton).

Piketty, Thomas (2014) *Capital in the Twenty-first Century* (Boston, MA: Harvard University Press).

Pilger, John (2012) 'Julia Gillard is no feminist hero', *The Guardian*, 15 October 2012; www.theguardian.com/commentisfree/2012/oct/15/julia-gillard-no-feminist-hero, accessed 14 December 2014.

Pinker, Steven (2012) *The Better Angels of our Nature: A History of Violence and Humanity* (London: Penguin).

Rees, Martin (2011) 'Are we all doomed?', *New Statesman*, 6 June 2011: 23.

Rees, Martin (2012) 'Even the theory of everything has limits', *The Telegraph* (UK), 19–25 September 2012: 26.

Reyes-Centenoa, Hugo, Silvia Ghirottob, Florent Détroitc, Dominique Grimaud-Hervéc, Guido Barbujanib and Katerina Harvati (2014) 'Genomic and cranial phenotype data support multiple modern human dispersals from Africa and a southern route into Asia', *Proceedings of the National Academy of Sciences of the United States of America* 111.20; www.pnas.org/content/111/20/7248.

Robb, Graham (2007) *The Discovery of France: A Historical Geography* (London: W.W. Norton).

Roberts, Yvonne (2014) 'In the Public Interest: The Role of the Modern State' (London: The Centre for Labour and Social Studies [Class]; classonline.org.uk/docs/2014_The_role_of_the_state_-_Yvonne_Roberts_FINAL.pdf).

Ruggie, John G. (ed.) (2008) *Embedding Global Markets: An Enduring Challenge* (Farnham, UK: Ashgate).

Ruggie, John G. (2013) 'Remarks at Opening Plenary UN Global Compact Leaders Forum by John G. Ruggie, Harvard University, Former UN Special Representative for Business and Human Rights, New York, 20 September 2013'; www.hks.harvard.edu/m-rcbg/CSRI/RuggieGCOpeningPlenarySept2013.pdf, accessed 27 November 2014.

Rusbridger, Alan, and Ewen MacAskill (2014) 'Edward Snowden Interview: The Edited Transcript', *The Guardian*, 18 July 2014; www.theguardian.com/world/2014/jul/18/-sp-edward-snowden-nsa-whistleblower-interview-transcript, accessed 28 November 2014.

Sagan, Carl 'Who Speaks for Earth?' [video], *YouTube*, bit.ly/1b7rSLF, accessed 5 February 2014.

Said, Edward W. (1979) *Orientalism* (London: Vintage).

Schmidheiny, Stephan, and the Business Council for Sustainable Development (1992) *Changing Course: A Global Business Perspective on Development and the Environment* (Cambridge, MA: MIT Press).

Self, Will (2013a) 'Picture This', *New Statesman*, 22–28 March 2013: 51.

Self, Will (2013b) 'Fail Better', *The Observer*, 22 June 2013: Review, 4.

Sheldrake, Rupert (2014) 'Earth Talk: Science and Spiritual Practices' [video], *YouTube*; bit.ly/1yORnui, accessed 13 March 2014.

Smith, Adam (1759) *The Theory of Moral Sentiments* (London: Penguin Classics, 2013).

Smith, Adam (1776) *An Inquiry into the Nature and Causes of the Wealth of Nations* (New York: Bantam Classics, 2003).

Sontag, Susan (1993) *Writing Itself: On Roland Barthes – A Reader* (London: Vintage).

Sorkin, Andrew Ross (2009) *Too Big to Fail: Inside the Battle to Save Wall Street (London: Viking)*.

Stiglitz, Joseph (2014) 'Mired in Malaise: Stiglitz on Martin Wolf', *Financial Times*, 30–31 August 2014: 8.

Stoll, Mark (2012) 'Rachel Carson's *Silent Spring*: A Book That Changed the World'; www.environmentandsociety.org/exhibitions/silent-spring/personal-attacks-rachel-carson, accessed 4 August 2014.

Strategy& (2012) 'The Third Billion: As growing numbers of women enter the economic mainstream, they will have a profound effect on global business', Strategy&; www.strategyand.pwc.com/global/home/what-we-think/third_billion, accessed 1 December 2014.

Swilling, Mark, and Eve Annecke (2012) *Just Transitions: Explorations of Sustainability in an Unfair World* (United Nations University Press).

Tekelova, Mira (2014) 'Adair Turner. The Clearest Explanation of the Cause of Financial Crisis', Positive Money, 7 November 2012; www.positivemoney.org/2012/11/adair-turner-the-clearest-explanation-of-the-cause-of-financial-crisis, accessed 2 December 2014.

Tench, Watkin (1789) *1788* (Melbourne: Text Publishing, 2009).

Tett, Gillian (2013) 'Central Banking: Still a Man's World', *FT.com/magazine*, 10–11 August 2013.

Tóibín, Colm (2012) *The Testament of Mary* (London: Penguin).

Toynbee, Arnold (1972) 'Foreword', in *A Study of History: The First Abridged One-Volume Edition – Illustrated* (Oxford, UK: Oxford University Press).

United Nations Secretary-General's High-Level Panel on Global Sustainability (2012) *Resilient People, Resilient Planet: A Future Worth Choosing* (New York: United Nations).

Viereck, George Sylvester (1929) 'What Life Means to Einstein: An Interview by George Sylvester Viereck', *The Saturday Evening Post*, 26 October 1929: 117

Waddell, Steve (2011) *Global Action Networks: Creating Our Future Together* (London: Palgrave Macmillan).

Waddock, Sandra (2008) *The Difference Makers: How Social and Institutional Entrepreneurs Created the Corporate Responsibility Movement* (Sheffield, UK: Greenleaf Publishing).

Waddock, Sandra, and Malcolm McIntosh (2012) *SEE Change: Making the Transition to a Sustainable Enterprise Economy* (Sheffield, UK: Greenleaf Publishing).

Ward, Barbara (1966) *Spaceship Earth* (New York: Columbia University Press).

Wilkinson, Richard, and Kate Pickett (2010) *The Spirit Level: Why Equality is Better for Everyone* (London: Penguin).

Winston, Robert (2013) 'The New Statesman Centenary Questionnaire', *New Statesman*, 1–7 November 2013: 70.

World Commission on Environment and Development (1987) *Our Common Future* ('The Brundtland Report'; Oxford, UK: Oxford University Press).

Zander, Rosamund, and Benjamin Zander (2000) *The Art of Possibility: Transforming Professional and Personal Life* (Boston, MA: Harvard Business School Press).

Žižek, Slavoj (2010) 'Wake Up and Smell the Apocalypse', *New Scientist*, 28 August 2010: 28.

Žižek, Slavoj (2011) *Living in the End Times* (London: Verso).

Index

Also by Malcolm McIntosh

- Japan Re-Armed (Bloomsbury Academic Collections, 1986 and 2013, ISBN 978-1-78093-513-3).
- Managing Britain's Defence (Macmillan, 1990, ISBN 978-0-333-48075-5).
- Good Business? Case Studies in Corporate Social Responsibility (editor) (SAUS Guides & Reports; Policy Press, 1993, ISBN 978-1-873575-58-1).
- Corporate Citizenship: Successful Strategies for Responsible Companies (with Deborah Leipziger, Keith A. Jones and Gill Coleman) (Financial Times/Prentice Hall, 1998, ISBN 978-0-273-63106-4).
- Perspectives on Corporate Citizenship (co-editor with Jörg Andriof) (Greenleaf Publishing, 2001, ISBN 978-1-874719-39-7).
- Global Companies in the Twentieth Century: Selected Archival Histories of BP, Rio Tinto, Royal Dutch Shell, BBC, Cable & Wireless, Marks & Spencer, BHP, Barclays Bank, Levi Strauss & Co. (co-editor with Ruth Thomas) (Routledge, 2001, ISBN 978-0-415-18110-5).
- Living Corporate Citizenship: Strategic Routes to Socially Responsible Business (with Deborah Leipziger, Ruth Thomas and Gill Coleman) (Financial Times/Prentice Hall, 2003, ISBN 978-0-273-65433-9).
- Something to Believe In. Creating Trust and Hope in Organisations: Stories of Transparency, Accountability and Governance (co-editor with Rupesh A. Shah and David F. Murphy) (Greenleaf Publishing, 2003, ISBN 978-1-874719-69-4).
- Raising a Ladder to the Moon: The Complexities of Corporate Social and Environmental Responsibility (Palgrave Macmillan, 2003, ISBN 978-0-333-96270-1).
- Learning To Talk: Corporate Citizenship and the Development of the UN Global Compact (co-editor with Sandra Waddock and Georg Kell) (Greenleaf Publishing, 2004, ISBN 978-1-874719-75-5).
- Corporate Citizenship in Africa: Lessons from the Past; Paths to the Future (co-editor with Wayne Visser and Charlotte Middleton) (Greenleaf Publishing, 2006, ISBN 978-1-874719-55-7).
- New Perspectives on Human Security (co-editor with Alan Hunter) (Greenleaf Publishing, 2010, ISBN 978-1-906093-41-9).
- SEE Change: Making the Transition to a Sustainable Enterprise Economy (with Sandra Waddock) (Greenleaf Publishing, 2011, ISBN 978-1-906093-45-7).
- The Necessary Transition: The Journey towards the Sustainable Enterprise Economy (editor) (Greenleaf Publishing, 2013, ISBN 978-1-906093-89-1).
- Business, Capitalism and Corporate Citizenship: A Collection of

Seminal Essays (editor) (Greenleaf Publishing, 2015 [forthcoming], ISBN 978-1-78353-499-9).

- **Globalization, Corporate Citizenship and the non-European Gaze: A Collection of Seminal Essays** (editor) (Greenleaf Publishing, 2015 [forthcoming], ISBN 978-1-78353-496-8).